VOLUME ONE HUNDRED AND FIVE

ADVANCES IN
COMPUTERS

Advances in
COMPUTERS

Edited by

ATIF M. MEMON
College Park, MD,
United States

ACADEMIC PRESS

An imprint of Elsevier

elsevier.com

Academic Press is an imprint of Elsevier
50 Hampshire Street, 5th Floor, Cambridge, MA 02139, United States
525 B Street, Suite 1800, San Diego, CA 92101-4495, United States
The Boulevard, Langford Lane, Kidlington, Oxford OX5 1GB, United Kingdom
125 London Wall, London, EC2Y 5AS, United Kingdom

First edition 2017

ISBN: 978-0-12-812232-7
ISSN: 0065-2458

For information on all Academic Press publications
visit our website at https://www.elsevier.com/books-and-journals

Working together
to grow libraries in
developing countries

www.elsevier.com • www.bookaid.org

Publisher: Zoe Kruze
Acquisition Editor: Zoe Kruze
Editorial Project Manager: Shellie Bryant
Production Project Manager: Surya Narayanan Jayachandran
Senior Cover Designer: Greg Harris

Typeset by SPi Global, India

CONTENTS

PREFACE

This volume of *Advances in Computers* is the 105th in this series. This series, which has been continuously published since the 1960s, presents in each volume four to seven chapters describing new developments in software, hardware, or uses of computers. I invite leaders in their respective fields of computing to contribute a chapter about recent advances.

Volume 105 focuses on four important topics. Chapter 1, entitled "Web-Based Behavioral Modeling for Continuous User Authentication," by Dr. Leslie C. Milton discusses the important role that authentication plays in how we interact with today's computers, mobile devices, and the web. This topic has become especially important because in recent years more corporate information and applications have become accessible via the Internet. Many employees are working from remote locations and need access to secure corporate files. During this time, it is possible for malicious or unauthorized users to gain access to the system. For this reason, it is logical to have some mechanism in place to detect whether the logged-in user is the same user in control of the user's session. Therefore, highly secure authentication methods must be used. In this chapter, the author posits that each user is unique in their use of computer systems. It is this uniqueness that is leveraged to "continuously authenticate users" while they use web software. To monitor user behavior, *n*-gram models are used to capture user interactions with web-based software. This statistical language model essentially captures sequences and subsequences of user actions, their orderings, and temporal relationships that make them unique by providing a model of how each user typically behaves. Users are then continuously monitored during software operations. Large deviations from "normal behavior" can possibly indicate malicious or unintended behavior. This approach is implemented in a system called Intruder Detector that models user actions as embodied in web logs generated in response to a user's actions.

In Chapter 2, "Advances in Model-Based Testing of GUI-Based Software," Dr. Ishan Banerjee describes that the all-too-familiar Graphical User Interface (GUI) has become an integral component of today's software. A stable and reliable GUI is necessary for correct functioning of software applications. Comprehensive verification of the GUI is a routine part of most software development life cycles. The input space of a GUI is typically large, making exhaustive verification difficult. GUI defects are often revealed by exercising parts of the GUI that interact with each other. In recent years, model-based methods that target specific GUI interactions have been developed. These methods create a formal model of the GUI's input space from specification of the GUI, visible GUI behaviors, static analysis of the GUI's program code, and dynamic analysis of interactions between the GUI and its program code. This chapter discusses recent advances in testing GUI-based software. It describes techniques that generate test cases for GUI-based applications. Some popular methods are described, specifically ones that create a model of the GUI and generate test cases based on the GUI model.

In Chapter 3, "Fault Localization Using Hybrid Static/Dynamic Analysis," Dr. Ethar Elsaka notes that the increasing complexity of today's software makes the software development process highly time and resource consuming. The increasing number of software configurations, input parameters, usage scenarios, supporting platforms, external dependencies, and versions plays an important role in expanding the costs of maintaining and repairing unforeseeable software faults. To repair software faults, developers spend considerable time in identifying the scenarios, leading to those faults and root-causing the problems. While software debugging remains largely manual, it is not the case with software testing and verification. The chapter discusses ways to improve the software development process in general, and software debugging process in particular, by devising techniques and methods for automated software debugging, which leverage the advances in automatic test case generation and replay. In particular, novel algorithms are devised to discover faulty execution paths in programs by utilizing already existing software test cases, which can be either automatically or manually generated. The execution traces or, alternatively, the sequence covers of the failing test cases are extracted. Afterward, commonalities between these test case sequence covers are extracted, processed, analyzed, and presented to the developers in the form of subsequences that may be causing the fault. The idea behind this approach is that code sequences that are shared between a number of faulty test cases for the same reason resemble the faulty execution path, and hence, the search space for the faulty execution path can be narrowed down by using a large number of test cases. To achieve this goal, an efficient algorithm is implemented for finding common subsequences among a set of code sequence covers. Optimization techniques are devised to generate shorter and more logical sequence covers and to select subsequences with high likelihood of containing the root cause among the set of all possible common subsequences.

A hybrid static/dynamic analysis approach is designed to trace back the common subsequences from the end to the root cause.

In Chapter 4, "Characterizing Software Test Case Behavior With Regression Models," Dr. Bryan Robbins notes that testing modern software applications, such as those built on an event-driven paradigm, requires effective consideration of context. Model-based testing (MBT) approaches have been presented as an effective way to consider context, but effective MBT requires a high level of automation. Fully automated approaches too often lead to issues that threaten the very claims that MBT offers, such as generating test cases that are not fully executable and generating very large suites of test cases. This chapter describes a new class of models for automated MBT workflows, called predictive regression models. The work compares these models with those in a state-of-the-art automated MBT workflow. It then describes a modern infrastructure tor execute large MBT suites, to counter the seed suite required to construct predictive regression models, and to further enable effective MBT approaches in general. The chapter concludes with a summary of recent research which effectively applied a regression model for test case feasibility as a filter for automatically generated test cases.

I hope that you find these articles of interest. If you have any suggestions of topics for future chapters, or if you wish to be considered as an author for a chapter, I can be reached at atif@cs.umd.edu.

Prof. A.M. Memon, PhD,

College Park,

MD, United States

## CHAPTER ONE

Web-Based Behavioral Modeling for Continuous User Authentication (CUA)

L.C. Leonard
U.S. Army Engineer Research and Development Center, Vicksburg, MS, United States

Contents

Abstract

Authentication plays an important role in how we interact with computers, mobile devices, the web, etc. For example, in recent years, more corporate information and applications have been accessible via the Internet and Intranet. Many employees are working from remote locations and need access to secure corporate files. During this time, it is possible for malicious or unauthorized users to gain access to the system. For this reason, it is logical to have some mechanism in place to detect whether the logged-in user is the same user in control of the user's session. Therefore, highly secure

Advances in Computers, Volume 105
ISSN 0065-2458
http://dx.doi.org/10.1016/bs.adcom.2016.12.001

authentication methods must be used. We posit that each of us is unique in our use of computer systems. It is this uniqueness that is leveraged to "continuously authenticate users" while they use web software. To monitor user behavior, n-gram models are used to capture user interactions with web-based software. This statistical language model essentially captures sequences and subsequences of user actions, their orderings, and temporal relationships that make them unique by providing a model of how each user typically behaves. Users are then continuously monitored during software operations. Large deviations from "normal behavior" can possibly indicate malicious or unintended behavior. This approach is implemented in a system called *Intruder Detector* (*ID*) that models user actions as embodied in web logs generated in response to a user's actions. User identification through web logs is cost-effective and nonintrusive. For these experiments, we use two classification techniques; binary and multiclass classification.

1. INTRODUCTION

Many web-based applications rely on authentication methods that are reliable, convenient and secure. Username and password have been universally accepted by most applications to be the only form of authentication. Some systems require the use of long passwords that need to be changed frequently. They can be difficult to remember, create, and manage [1]. In addition to long passwords, passwords that are too short or lack complexity also pose a significant risk. In a study of over 3.3 million leaked passwords from North America and Western Europe, SplashData records "123456" and "password" as the top two passwords chosen by users [2].

Conventional authentication methods do not ask the user to verify their identity during their active log-in session, leaving the computer system vulnerable to malicious or unintended use while the user is logged-in [3]. To improve the authentication process for web-based applications, there must be a method to continuously verify the identity of a user. *Continuous User Authentication* (CUA) has been proven to solve this limitation. CUA techniques monitor, verify, and authenticate users during their entire session. CUA generates user profiles and compares them to the user's stored profile. If user activity deviates from its normal pattern of usage, the system generates an alarm. CUA systems have user profiles that are customized for every application. This makes it difficult for attackers to know which actions will be detected as intrusive [4].

Several studies have used biometrics to continuously authenticate users by the use of cognitive fingerprints, eye scans, color of user's clothing, and face tracking [3,5,6]. However, many of these techniques require additional hardware and cost to operate efficiently. Behavioral modeling addresses these limitations by monitoring how users interact with the system. Evaluating mouse movement, how users search for and select information, and the habitual typing rhythm of users are measures used to continuously observe a user's behavior [7,8]. Although these approaches do not require special hardware, most of them require the installation of specialized monitoring software.

This chapter addresses challenges that occur when modeling the behavior of users that interact with web-based organizational information system applications. These applications run inside a web browser-based front-end and are accessible via hypertext transfer protocol (HTTP). It also includes middleware to implement business logic and a back-end database. We categorize information system as organized systems for the collection, organization, communication, and storage of information [9]. We develop a new tool, *Intruder Detector* (*ID*), to model unique behavioral foot prints for each user. Patterns of use for a specific user or group of users is captured in this footprint and leveraged to "continuously" authenticate the user. *ID* performs behavioral analysis for each user and builds a context of each user's behavior, based on a statistical language model, to verify the user's identity. No additional hardware is required to deploy this tool. Furthermore, we seek to provide a cost-effective and nonintrusive solution for web-based user authentication. Our preliminary work for this chapter received the Best Paper Award at the *Eighth International Conference on Emerging Security Information, Systems, and Technologies* [10].

We provide the following contributions from the work reported in this chapter:

- We develop a novel keyword abstraction technique to preprocess large volumes of web logs by eliminating incomplete, noisy, and inconsistent data.
- We use statistical language models to capture the behavior of users, while they interact with organizational web-based applications.
- We develop a continuous user authentication framework with the ability to categorize user sessions into a predefined set of roles or finer-grained user profiles. This framework is also used to identify outliers in role-based user behavior.
- We introduce a set of evaluation metrics to test the feasibility of our approach.

1.1 Continuous User Authentication Scenarios

This work explores how modeling user behavior affects system security and usability when using data that is already available (e.g., web server logs). The following two scenarios show how CUA may be used in typical settings.

Scenario 1: *Alice* uses her laptop to *telework* from a local coffee shop. She uses her web browser to login to her corporate site and perform her daily tasks. As she steps away from her laptop to get a refill of coffee, an unauthorized person accesses her laptop to perform actions on the corporate site, maliciously merging and changing sensitive records. Unbeknownst to the "intruder," the website is equipped with our CUA system, called *Intruder Detector*, that automatically detects deviations from normal behavior and subsequently locks her computer. *ID* works as follows: It monitors all user actions and builds, for each user, an *n*-gram model[a], a mathematical representation of how the user typically interacts with the web application. *ID* determines, in real time, whether the user is deviating from expected behavior, signaling the possible presence of an intruder. Because this instance of *ID* is based solely on analysis of web logs, it is extremely fast and it requires no special hardware or changes to the web application.

Scenario 2: *Bob's* office computer is used to perform illegal transactions via the company's web application. Because the computer is located in a "secure" area, the forensics team concludes that the malicious transactions must have been done by a coworker. They retrieve the system's web access logs and filter out those that originated from *Bob's* computer, thereby obtaining all the web requests between *Bob's* computer and the web server. They then use these logs and the models stored in *ID*, which represent exactly how each user typically behaves when using the web application, to pinpoint the coworker who most closely resembles the pattern of unauthorized accesses. In this scenario, there is some level of uncertainty because the malicious sequences by the intruder may or may not match their stored user model. At this point, *ID* is simply one tool in the investigative process, and additional forensic data is needed to pinpoint the person performing the malicious transactions.

---

[a] An *n*-gram representation models sequences using the statistical properties of *n*-grams (contiguous sequences of *n* items/actions).

1.2 Approach

We analyze how log data from web-based applications can be used to predict user behavior. Web server logs capture all requests made to the server. For many systems, web server log files are not fully utilized. These logs, also called access logs, include historical information about the activities performed by users. There are several ways web server logs can be used to present valuable information to a system administrator. For example, information extracted from log files has been used by companies to provide better service to customers and improve the quality of their website.

In addition to improving user interaction, web logs can be used to trace patterns of behavior. The patterns can then be used with statistical language models, such as n-grams, to predict user behavior. n-gram models have performed surprisingly well in the domain of natural language processing (NLP), where researchers have found that a history of only one to two events is necessary to obtain optimal predictive capabilities [11]. An n-gram model captures all sequences of a fixed length, N, from previously observed user input, which allows prediction and evaluation of future behavior based on frequencies. In the realm of NLP, these sequences are words generated for sentences. Web-based user actions also have a grammar-like sequential structure. If it is assumed that the event sequences carried out by users of a software system are analogous to natural language, we would expect to find the same predictive power in n-gram models of software event sequences as well.

There are several NLP models that could be used for this work. For example, Hidden Markov Models (HMMs) are much more elaborate models with the ability to track independent probability distributions, including those of hidden variables. We explore several NLP models and determine that n-gram language models provide predictive power when modeling user behavior based on web logs. Understanding the behavior and utility of n-grams to build user profiles is a reasonable prerequisite for using more advanced machine learning methods.

This work addresses the following challenges and makes the following corresponding contributions to the realm of web-based user profile analysis:

Challenge 1: Several models exist for the analysis of user behavior.

Contribution 1: In this work, we explore several statistical language models.

We successfully identify a suitable model for web-based usage behavior.

Challenge 2: There is no straightforward method to identify the behavior of users that interact with web-based applications.

Contribution 2: We develop a novel keyword abstraction process to identify user activity for each system user.

Challenge 3: It is complex to monitor user behavior without the use of specialized hardware.

Contribution 3: We develop new techniques to monitor user behavior of web-based applications using information that is already available to a system administrator.

Challenge 4: There is a trade-off in performance when developing a CUA system.

Contribution 4: We test the performance of our implementation using a large set of evaluation metrics to access the feasibility of our approach.

Our final contribution is an empirical analysis of the CUA technique. This method is applied to a government fielded training support website. Over a period of 3 years, approximately 4000 users, with one of four access levels, were captured in the dataset.

1.3 Scope of Work

There are several types of web-based information systems. In this work, to provide focus, we only consider web-based organizational information system applications described in Fig. 1[b]. These systems include executive, senior, middle, and worker-level access usage. To access these applications, employees must use the organization's network with an option to connect via virtual private network. Modeling common websites without an organizational focus, such as www.amazon.com, are beyond the focus of this study.

1.4 Broader Impact

We believe the work presented in this chapter will provide an increased level of security when combined with existing authentication techniques (e.g., passwords, biometrics) to support many demands of today's computing environment. While conducting this work, we have witnessed how important it is to evaluate user behavior and provide a secure environment for our users to conduct their day-to-day business. After reviewing the web logs for this study, we identified several IP addresses that was not indicative of the interaction of approved users. This prompted the information assurance

---

[b] https://en.wikipedia.org/wiki/Information_system.

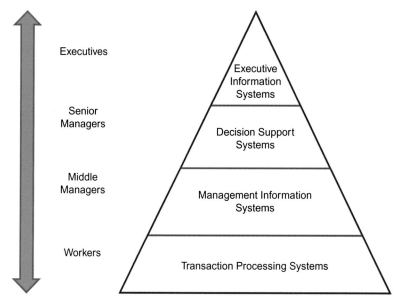

Fig. 1 Organizational-level information management systems.

team to launch an investigation and put measures in place to stop this activity. In this case, *ID* could have been utilized to identify and stop interactions that do not closely resemble stored usage profiles.

Besides its importance to the realm of security, modeling user behavior, in general, is an important process for the customization and adaptation of user-specific needs[c]. Dynamic user modeling gives a current picture of how the user interacts with the software. As a user's interest and behavior changes over time, adaptive learning can be applied to increase the predictive power of the models. This is needed for CUA to be effective in this domain. We believe *n*-grams are highly effective models that can be used to capture user interactions as sequences by aiding in the identification of patterns that deviate from normal behavior.

1.5 Chapter Outline

The remainder of this chapter is organized as follows. In Section 2, we present background and related work for statistical language models and continuous user authentication. Section 3 highlights the approach and contributions of our work. Specifically, we show how *Intruder Detector* is

---

[c] http://en.wikipedia.org/wiki/User_modeling.

used in typical settings and the valued-added for this approach. Finally, Section 4 presents the conclusion and areas for future work.

2. BACKGROUND

In this section, classical forms of authentication described to understand the need for nonintrusive, continuous authentication methods. Several existing approaches in the CUA domain have been evaluated. However, this work focuses on the use of Statistical Language Models (SLM) to capture sequential behavior of users that interact with web-based organizational information systems. A survey of these techniques is outlined to add context to this study.

2.1 Classical Authentication Methods

Various authentication methods exist. Passwords, smart cards, digital certificates, Kerberos, and biometrics are among the many authentication methods currently employed. There are three classical forms of authentication: (1) something the user knows, e.g., password, pin; (2) something the user has, e.g., smart card, Yubikey [12]; and (3) something the user is, e.g., iris scan, fingerprint.

These authentication mechanisms are useful but have well-known limitations. A single point-of-failure exists if a user's password is compromised and later accessed by a malicious user. In addition, the patterns used when creating a password warrants some concern because keystroke analysis indicates that users often resort to special patterns [13]. If a device is found unlocked or hijacked during a user session, the system becomes compromised. Many biometric techniques also require additional hardware to collect data. Biometrics is not secret [14]. Intruders can observe a user's features and attempt to manipulate the system. Many companies and organizations use multifactor authentication (MFA) to mitigate this risk. MFA uses two or more classical forms of authentication to gain access to the system. If one form of authentication is cracked, guessed, or otherwise stolen, an attacker's access is still prohibited.

Various studies have explored the use of authentication. Kaminsky *et al.* address challenges for user authentication in a global file system [15]. This approach uses an authentication server to identify users based on local information. Researchers of cloud computing security methods have developed implicit authentication to identify a user's past behavior to authenticate mobile devices [16]. These two studies have one major limitation worth noting. They lack the ability to continuously monitor a user's behavior as they interact with the system.

2.2 Defining Continuous User Authentication

Cybersecurity has become a key concern for many organizations and companies. For example, the Office of Personnel Management informed millions of government and military employees that their personal information may be compromised [17]. For many systems, the first line of defense is authentication. Google and DARPA agree that elaborate password rules must be abandon and the use of strong authentication should be used to avoid impersonations [18,19].

Authentication techniques are usually performed at the beginning of a user session. This form of one-time validation is ineffective in preventing malicious and unintended use. For web applications, a password and username combination for authentication has historically been used in the context of a person's initial encounter with a computer system. Over 20 years ago, when e-commerce and secure web was first introduced, passwords were mainly a stopgap measure. It was expected that something better would replace it soon. As applications and devices evolve, this means of authentication is becoming insufficient. CUA fills this gap by transparently monitoring user activity in an effort to identify deviations from normal workflow patterns. These patterns are stored usage profiles of each user of the system. Fig. 2 provides a simple description of how a system equipped with CUA will work. The user is asked for traditional authentication credentials (i.e., username/password) to enter the application. After successful authentication, the user begins interacting with the system. The user is asked to reauthenticate if current interactions deviate from stored usage profiles. CUA adds an additional form of end-user authentication; something you do (e.g., typical patterns of behavior).

A robust CUA system has the following basic characteristics [20]:

- *Continual*: Reauthentication should be performed periodically to check if the current user is the logged-in user.
- *Nonintrusive*: Intrusive authentication hinders usability and provides a negative experience for the user. Therefore, the system must provide a seamless, nonintrusive user-friendly environment.
- *Behavioral*: The system must extract behavioral attributes from normal user operations. These attributes should be cost-effective and have unique usage profiles for each user.

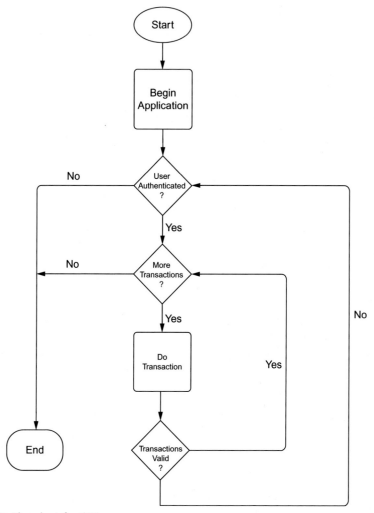

Fig. 2 Flowchart for CUA.

2.3 Existing Continuous User Authentication Techniques

The realm of CUA has been extensively evaluated with the use of biometrics. One study uses cognitive fingerprints to measure computational behavior by means of computational linguistics and structural semantic analysis [19]. This study uses a combination of metrics that include eye scans and keystrokes to evaluate how the user searches for and selects information. In addition, a number of CUA studies use one or more hard and soft biometric traits to continuously authenticate a user. Niinuma *et al.* propose a

CUA framework to automatically register the color of a user's clothing and their face as soft biometric traits [3,5]. Results from this study show that the system is able to successfully authenticate the user with high tolerance to the user's posture. Limitations to these studies exist because of the additional hardware that is needed to implement this technique which can become costly if an entire organization uses this feature to authenticate users.

Monrose *et al.* propose an authentication method that uniquely identifies users based on the analysis of keystrokes [8]. Keystroke dynamics focuses on how you type vs what you type. The habitual typing rhythm of a user is a function of the user and their environment. Therefore, limitations to this approach occur when the user is faced with environmental factors that affect their typing pattern. Altinok *et al.* propose a continuous biometric authentication system that provides an estimate of authentication certainty at any given time, even in the absence of any biometric data [21]. In this case, the authentication uncertainty increases over time which leads to a decrease in system usability. In a similar study, Kang *et al.* introduce temporal integration of biometrics and behavioral features to continuously authenticate users [22].

A face tracking system that uses color and edge information is used to compute behavioral features. Shen *et al.* use mouse dynamics when implementing continuous user authentication [7]. This technique is used to observe behavioral features in mouse operations to detect malicious users. However, there are some existing limitations with this emerging approach. Behavioral variability occurs because of human or environmental factors. For example, if the user switches software environments or experiences biological or emotional change, the user's behavior will be modified significantly. Such changes could possibly identify the user as an impostor. Xie *et al.* use a notable approach to identify legitimate users early when using online services by implementing a vouching process without the use of biometrics [23]. They introduce a system, Souche, to monitor vouching via social communities (i.e., Twitter, Email). Souche is effective in identifying 85% of legitimate users and denying admission of malicious users. Our work seeks to solve similar issues without the presence of social communities.

In recent years, mobile devices have been used to learn user behavior. Researchers introduced SenSec as a mobile framework to collect sensory data to construct a gesture model of how a user interacts with a mobile device [24]. Similar to our work, n–grams are used to capture user patterns. The SenSec system achieves over 70% accuracy in user classification and authentication tasks. In addition, Saevanee *et al.* use multimodel biometric techniques with mobile devices using linguistic profiling, keystroke dynamics and behavioral profiling for user authentication [25]. Results from this study show a 91% reduction rate in the number of intrusive authentication requests.

This body-of-work extends beyond the aforementioned studies in the following ways:

1. Instead of using traditional biometric traits, the possibility of using log information that is naturally generated by web applications to improve usability through nonintrusive, transparent authentication is explored.
2. This approach, integrated into a tool, uses a novel and simple n-gram language model to capture user behavior.
3. Experiments are based on data from actual users of a fielded Department of Defense (DOD) system who are completing day-to-day tasks.

2.4 Statistical Language Modeling

In this work, we use SLM to classify users. This modeling technique has been successfully implemented for a variety of language-based technologies. Document classification [26], information retrieval [27], machine translation [28], and speech recognition [29] all rely on this modeling technique. Many of these models decompose the probability of a sentence into a product of conditional probabilities [30]

$$
\begin{aligned}
P\left(w_1^n\right) &= P(w_1)P(w_2|w_1)P(w_3|w_1^2)...P(w_n|w_1w_2...w_{n-1}) \\
&= P(w_1)P(w_2|w_1)P(w_3|w_1^2)...P\left(w_n|w_1^{n-1}\right) \\
&= \prod_{k=1}^{n} P\left(w_k|w_1^{k-1}\right),
\end{aligned}
\tag{1}
$$

where w_k is the kth element in the sequence, and w^{k-1} $\{w_1, w_2, w_3, ..., w_n, ...\}$ is the *history, h*. Table 1 summarizes the SLMs explored in this work. The following sections provide more detail on each technique.

2.4.1 Neural Networks

Neural networks, also referred to as artificial neural networks, for machine learning and cognitive science, were inspired by biological neural networks. Neural network models have demonstrated success in pattern recognition [31], financial modeling [32], biomedicine [33], etc. This model uses interconnected *neurons* for communication. Each connection has adaptive

Table 1 Statistical Language Models

Model	Technique	Section
Statistical language models	Neural networks	2.4.1
	Maximum entropy	2.4.2
	Probabilistic context-free grammars	2.4.3
	Decision trees	2.4.4
	n-grams	2.4.5
	Hidden Markov models	2.4.6

weights that are tuned by a learning algorithm (supervised and unsupervised). Continuous-valued features are used to automatically learn as a function of the history [34]. Artificial neurons perform the following task:

1. Receive signals from other neurons in the network.
2. Multiply each signal by the corresponding connection strength (e.g., adaptive weight).
3. Take the sum of the weighted signals and send them to an activation function.
4. Send output to other neurons in the network.

Topology and operational mode of neural networks vary in literature. However, the most common configuration is to employ the use of an *input layer, hidden layer,* and *output layer* as shown in Fig. 3. The number of input nodes at the input layer is determined by feature values or independent variables. The output nodes are dependent on the number of classes or values to predict. To date, there is no optimal method to determine hidden nodes. If a network does not have enough hidden nodes, the input and output mappings will not be learned well. On the other hand, if there are too may hidden nodes, the network will generalize poorly on unseen elements. When neural networks operate using probability, true incremental learning is achieved. New training data can be added without retraining the entire network model [35]. A novel neural network language model is described using the following equation [36]:

$$P(w|h) = \frac{e^{\sum_{i=1}^{N} \lambda_i f_i(s, w)}}{\sum_w e^{\sum_{i=1}^{N} \lambda_i f_i(s, w)}}, \qquad (2)$$

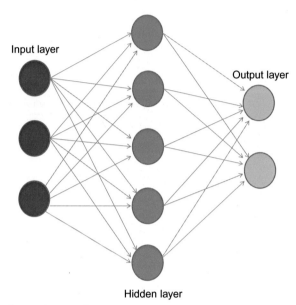

Fig. 3 Artificial neural network.

where e is the entropy value, f is a set of features, λ is a set of weights, h is the history, and s represents the state of the hidden layer. n-grams, N, are used as the learning algorithm in Eq. (2).

Jagadeesan *et al.* use a feed forward neural network with a backward propagation method to continuously authenticate users. This implementation is based on keyboard and mouse attributes. They use the k-nearest neighbor algorithm for classification. Experiments with application-based user reauthentication performed at 96.4% accuracy and 3.6% false alarms. For application-independent user reauthentication, the system performed at 82%. All experiments were conducted for relatively small data sets (i.e., five users).

2.4.2 Maximum Entropy
Entropy represents the lack-of-order or predictability. The *Principle of Maximum Entropy* is the correct distribution of $P(a, b)$ which maximizes *uncertainty* (i.e., entropy) based on constraints. By taking this approach, bias and assumptions are eliminated. For example, if we examine the conditional probability distribution for $P(y|x)$, then the conditional entropy is as follows:

$$H(Y|X) = -\sum_{x,y} P(x, y) \log \frac{P(x, y)}{P(y)} \tag{3}$$

$H(Y|X)$ is the entropy of random variable Y, given the value of another random variable, X, is known [37]. When using the *Principle of Maximum Entropy*, information from many sources can be combined into one language model. Such sources can originate from n-grams with history information or local information. Rosenfeld *et al.* use maximum entropy to create a single, combined model which captures information from various knowledge sources [38]. Each knowledge source represents a particular constraint. After constraints have been identified, a set of functions are created and the function with the highest entropy (i.e., uncertainty) is chosen. This adaptive approach to maximum entropy language modeling shows approximately 39% perplexity[d] when trained on the Wall Street Journal corpus.

2.4.3 Probabilistic Context-Free Grammars

Context-free grammars consist of terminals $(w^1, w^2, ..., w^V)$, nonterminals $(N^1, N^2, ..., N^n)$, a start symbol (N^1), and rules. Terminal symbols represent context that appear in the strings generated by the grammar. Nonterminal symbols are placeholders for patterns of terminal symbols that can be generated by nonterminals. A start symbol must be used as a special nonterminal to appear during the initial string generation. Rules are used to replace nonterminals in a string with other terminals/nonterminals.

$$
\begin{aligned}
\langle \text{Start} \rangle &\Rightarrow X = \langle \text{expression} \rangle \\
\langle \text{expression} \rangle &\Rightarrow \text{number} \\
\langle \text{expression} \rangle &\Rightarrow (\langle \text{expression} \rangle) \\
\langle \text{expression} \rangle &\Rightarrow \langle \text{expression} \rangle + \langle \text{expression} \rangle \\
\langle \text{expression} \rangle &\Rightarrow \langle \text{expression} \rangle - \langle \text{expression} \rangle \\
\langle \text{expression} \rangle &\Rightarrow \langle \text{expression} \rangle * \langle \text{expression} \rangle \\
\langle \text{expression} \rangle &\Rightarrow \langle \text{expression} \rangle / \langle \text{expression} \rangle
\end{aligned}
\tag{4}
$$

Expressions in Eq. (4) are an example of a context-free grammar. This grammar is used to form a mathematical expression with five terminals as operators $(+, -, *, /)$ and numbers. (*expression*) is the start symbol and the only nonterminal for this grammar. Suppose we want to find the correct grammar to generate $X = 45 + 98 * 4$ as a mathematical expression. The context-free string generation in Fig. 4 can be used.

---

[d] Perplexity measures how well a statistical language model predicts a sample set of data.

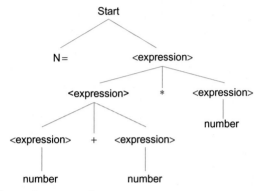

Fig. 4 Context-free string generation.

$$
\begin{array}{lc}
\text{Grammar} & \text{Probability} \\
\langle \text{Start} \rangle \Rightarrow X = \langle \text{expression} \rangle & 1.0 \\
\langle \text{expression} \rangle \Rightarrow \text{number} & 0.2 \\
\langle \text{expression} \rangle \Rightarrow (\langle \text{expression} \rangle) & 0.1 \\
\langle \text{expression} \rangle \Rightarrow \langle \text{expression} \rangle + \langle \text{expression} \rangle & 0.30 \\
\langle \text{expression} \rangle \Rightarrow \langle \text{expression} \rangle - \langle \text{expression} \rangle & 0.15 \\
\langle \text{expression} \rangle \Rightarrow \langle \text{expression} \rangle * \langle \text{expression} \rangle & 0.18 \\
\langle \text{expression} \rangle \Rightarrow \langle \text{expression} \rangle / \langle \text{expression} \rangle & 0.06
\end{array}
\tag{5}
$$

Probabilistic Context-free Grammars (PCFGs) assign probability estimates to each rule such that the sum of the probabilities for all rules expanding the same nonterminal is equal to one. For example, the grammar in Eq. (5) includes probabilities that should be used to generate an equation. If more than one trace through the grammar exists, the grammar with the highest probability is chosen. PCFGs can be learned from positive data examples alone but grammar induction is very difficult. This form of language modeling is robust and in some cases provides better predictive power than HMMs. PCFGs are biased toward smaller trees by making them more probable than trees with many traces.

2.4.4 Decision Trees

Decision trees were first applied to language modeling by Bahl *et al.* to estimate the probability of spoken words [39]. A single node is the starting point followed by binary questions that are asked as a method to arbitrarily partition the space of histories. As the space is partitioned, "leaves" are formed and training data is used to calculate the conditional probability of $P(w|h)$ for the next element. As the traversal continues, the questioning becomes more informative by the use of information theoretic metrics. Such metrics include *Kolomogorov Complexity, entropy, relative entropy, etc.* [40]. For example, if a person wants to assess how much it would cost to live in certain neighborhoods, the simplified decision tree in Fig. 5 could be used. The root node, *Location*, is evaluated with children nodes (*Neighborhood, price.isMod*) representing values for locations. The outputs for these logical tests are usually boolean values [41]. From Fig. 5, we derive: "If *location = city* ∧ *neighborhood = northside* ∧ *condition = excellent*, then the price for homes in this area is expensive."

Decision tree algorithms are primarily composed of training data, test data, a heuristic evaluation function, and a stopping criterion function. These models use recursion from the divide and conquer data structure to induce data from the root node downward. Ultimately, decision trees represent the "gold-standard" for partition-based models. However, size, complexity, and data sparseness lead to misclassification of elements when trees are large. To simplify the tree structure, Breslow and Aha provide five top-level categories for tree simplification as seen in Table 2 [41].

Petrovskiy uses a combination of decision tree classification and time-dependent features to learn user behavior for next-action prediction and anomaly detection from database logs generated by a banking Intranet

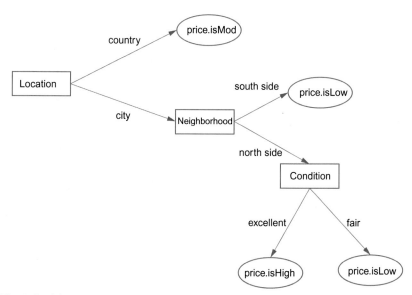

Fig. 5 Decision tree.

Table 2 Decision Tree Techniques

Simplification Approach	Procedures
Tree size control	Prepruning
	Postpruning
	Incremental resizing
Modify test space	Data-driven
	Hypothesis-driven
Modify test search	Selection measures
	Continuous features
	Lookahead search
Database restrictions	Case selection
	Feature selection
Alternative data structures	Decision graphs
	Rules

application [42]. Results show that decision trees have fair performance for next-action prediction and very little accuracy for anomaly detection.

2.4.5 n-*grams*

Markov models have been heavily used for their predictive power. Markov models assume that the probability of an occurring event is dependent only on the current state of a system. As a simple example, imagine that we would like to track the probability of a Sunny (S) day or Rainy (R) day of weather. To learn the probability of a Sunny day, we could observe days for some period of time (e.g., 10 days) and count the number of Sunny days observed, *nSunny*. Then, we could assign the likelihood of a Sunny day occurring to be $\frac{nSunny}{10}$. When waking up each morning, we assume that the probability of a Sunny day is given by this same fixed rate. Under this interpretation, to find $P\,(SSSSS)$ (i.e., five Sunny days in a row), we would simply solve $P\,(S)^5$. Probabilities are computed based on a set of observations. The observations can be mapped to a sequence of class labels $\{w_1, w_2, w_3, \ldots, w_n, \ldots\}$. In this sequence, w_1 represents the first observation, w_2 the second, and so on. The chain rule of probability theory computes the probability of an observation according to some prior context available at each data point. When using this method, the number of parameters grow exponentially with the number of observations in prior context. Therefore, it is not feasible to accurately estimate conditional probabilities. Instead of computing this type of probability, *n*-grams are used to approximate prior history by looking at the last few observations.

In most cases, it is reasonable to apply the *Markov assumption*, which assumes that the probability of observing w_i is only dependent on a very small set of preceding observations. Markov models make predictions on future elements without looking too far in the past. Therefore, *n*-gram models are Markov models which use $(N-1)$ elements of context to define the current state of the model [43]. These stochastic process models are mostly stationary since we are assuming past behavior is a good prediction of what will happen in the future. However, natural language is not stationary because the probability of upcoming words can be dependent on events that are arbitrarily distant and time dependent. Therefore, the statistical models of *n*-grams only give an approximation of the correct distributions and entropies of natural language. Constructing or training an *n*-gram model requires the ability to observe example sequences occurring in the domain to be modeled. To train a model well, single events from sequences in all relevant contexts must be observed. Studies reveal that low-order Markov models do not make accurate predictions because it does not look back far enough to past observations. Contrarily, many limitations exist for higher order models. Reduced coverage, high state-space complexity, and overall prediction accuracy are a few of the short comings of this approach. In response, Deshpande and Karypis introduce a technique to combine different order Markov models to lower the state-space complexity while increasing coverage and accuracy for web pages [44]. Their selective Markov model uses frequency, confidence, and error pruning to discard certain states across different order Markov models. Manavoglu *et al.* use a combination of maximum entropy mixture models and Markov models to model behavior of web users [45]. Both models have various strengths and weaknesses but when combined they are able to accurately identify and visualize specific user behavior patterns. In this work, we seek to understand the limitations that exist for high-order and low-order Markov (i.e., *n*-gram) models for user identification and the detection of outliers.

2.4.6 Hidden Markov Models

HMMs are Markov models whose process transitions between states in an unobservable path. However, output that is dependent on these states is visible. Basic theory behind HMM was published in a series of classical research papers [46–48]. HMMs have been conventionally applied to problems that require the recovery of data sequences that are not immediately observable. These models have been used for speech recognition, gene prediction, part-of-speech tagging, activity recognition, etc.

An HMM is characterized by the following [49]:

1. N represents the number of states, S, in the model. Individual states are denoted as $S = \{S_1, S_2, S_3, ..., S_n\}$ and the state at time, t, is q_t.
2. M represents the number of distinct observation symbols per state (e.g., discrete alphabet size). These symbols are denoted as $V = \{V_1, V_2, V_3, ..., V_M\}$ and correspond to the physical output of the modeled system.
3. Transition probability distribution for each state is denoted as $A = \{a_{ij}\}$.
4. B represents the observation symbol probability distribution in state j, $B = \{b_j (k)\}$, where $b_j (k) = P [V_k$ at $t|q_t = S_j]$.
5. π represents the initial state distribution where $\pi_i = P [q_1 = S_i]$.

To illustrate this model, we consider the weather as a concrete example. In Fig. 6, observable conditions are rainy, sunny, or cloudy conditions. Factors that influence these outcomes are hidden states (e.g., high and low pressure). The *start* state illustrates the initial probability of the model. On average, the model starts with *high* pressure at 70%. Transition probabilities are represented by the change in pressure in the underlying Markov chain. In this example, there is only a 40% chance that tomorrow has *low* pressure, if

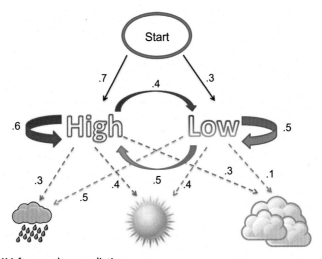

Fig. 6 HMM for weather prediction.

today's pressure is *high*. Probabilities for observable states represent the likelihood of a particular weather condition occurring. If we observe high pressure, there is a 40% chance it is sunny. To learn tasks, HMMs must find the best set of transition states and output probabilities using a maximum likelihood estimate.

3. INTRUDER DETECTOR: A TOOL FOR CUA

This section characterizes the application under evaluation (AUE). Specifically, we show the significance of modeling user behavior with *n*-grams. We also describe key contributions of this work. Each contribution provides the building blocks for the *Intruder Detector* tool.

3.1 Web-Based User Behavior Analysis

Modeling the behavior of users is an ongoing challenge in various application domains [50]. In web applications, obtaining a better knowledge of the user and purpose for the application is essential to provide an increased level of security. Applications in this study are based on organizational information systems. Such systems can be used for decision support, knowledge management, and e-learning. It is important to continuously monitor users as they interact with these systems. Insider threat, especially for decision support systems, can harm an organization's security practice, data, and computer system.

The web AUE for this work is a fielded government training support website, User Productivity Enhancement, Technology Transfer, and Training (PETTT) Online Knowledge Center (OKC), for the high performance computing (HPC) community. The PETTT activity is responsible for gathering the best ideas, algorithms, and software tools emerging from the national HPC infrastructure and making them available to the DOD and academic user community. This website is a repository of PETTT programmatic and technical information. It provides training course registration, course evaluation, information on several domain-specific areas and is a general source of information for its community of users. The system is a Java-based web application. Most pages are JavaServer Pages, with some servlets handling various tasks. The primary database utilizes Oracle 11 g enterprise edition. Xwiki Framework and Apache Struts are leveraged to give users with elevated privileges the ability to manage their own content. This portion of the system runs over a MySQL version 5.6.11 database. The operating system environment is Microsoft Server 2008 R2.

Users have the option to authenticate via two methods: Common Access Card (CAC) and Yubikey. The CAC is used to identify DOD civilian employees, Selected Reserve, active duty uniform service personnel, and government contractor personnel [51]. This card can also be used to gain physical access to buildings, controlled spaces, computer networks, and systems. The Yubikey is a key-sized device that is inserted into a user's computer system USB slot to provide an added layer of authentication. If users choose to login via Yubikey, they must enter a username and password. Finally, they are directed to touch the Yubikey to generate a random passcode to enter the web application. Fig. 7 presents a subset of pages that can be viewed by users of the AUE.

Each user account has one of the following associated roles; *User, Administrator (Admin), Management (Mgmt), Technologist (Tech)*. The *User* group has limited read access as well as the ability to enroll, evaluate, and register for courses. There are additional roles that provide access to areas of the system for administrative purposes (*Admin, Mgmt, Tech*). The most prominent of these is the Technologist role. These users interact with the system often as content administrators. Content administrators add updated data to the system, approve students for online training, arrange content, etc. Therefore,

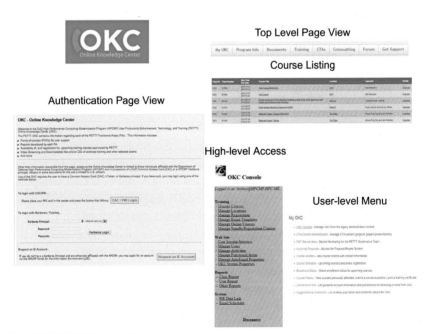

Fig. 7 PETTT OKC page view.

while we have more individual sessions available for the *User* role, the *Tech* role provides more keyword data. Users with the *Admin* role focus on technology/information integration, and data management as well as enhancements to the design and operation of PETTT OKC. The *Mgmt* role is reserved for those who provide oversight of the application. They are not very active users of this web application. *Tech* and *Admin* roles pose the greatest risk when access is unauthorized.

3.2 Feasibility Study

To provide an assessment of our approach, we analyze four preliminary models for the classification of role-based user data by observing the accuracy of *individual actions* (IA), *frequency of individual actions* (Freq-IA), *pairs of actions* (PA), and *frequency of pairs of actions* (Freq-PA). This data is obtained from the OKC web log files. It is our intuition that accuracy from these approaches will yield less than optimal results, and statistical language models, such as *n*-grams, must be used.

The data for each approach is partitioned into training and test set examples using the 90/10, 80/20, and 70/30 data split technique (training/test) as shown in Table 3. The data is sorted and placed into a training and test vector for comparison and classification. We compare the four preliminary approaches to *n*-gram models using the same partitioning. We run each experiment 10 times. For the evaluation of IA, we use binary numbers to identify matches in the vector. A "1" represents a keyword match and a "0" represents a mismatch. The ones are added and normalized by the size of the test set. Next, we evaluate PA. We would like to know if classification accuracy increases when pairs of keywords are used. We group training and testing sets as in the IA example using a Java HashMap data structure. If pairs are matched, the numerical key for the HashMap is increased until the entire set is evaluated. Finally, we divide the total number of matched pairs by the total number of pairs that exist in the test keyword dataset. Next, we observe classification accuracy for Freq-IA and Freq-PA. For each individual or keyword pair, we use a HashMap to count the number of times the keyword (or keyword pair) exist in the training and test dataset. If the frequency counts of the training and testing keyword pairs are within five, we classify the frequency as a match and add it to the classification accuracy.

Figs. 8–10 show role-based accuracy results for this feasibility study. It was our intuition that the use of individual keywords would yield the worst accuracy. In each data split, this accuracy is less than 10%. Classification of

Table 3 Number of Keywords and Sessions for Each Data Split

Data Split	Role	Sessions	Keywords
90/10	Management-train	247	5045
	Management-test	28	814
	Technologist-train	421	31,965
	Technologist-test	47	3709
	Admin-train	521	22,645
	Admin-test	58	3388
	User-train	1735	24,849
	User-test	193	2808
80/20	Management-train	220	4643
	Management-test	55	1216
	Technologist-train	374	28,629
	Technologist-test	94	7045
	Admin-train	463	20,298
	Admin-test	116	5735
	User-train	1542	21,949
	User-test	386	5708
70/30	Management-train	192	3787
	Management-test	83	2072
	Technologist-train	327	24,643
	Technologist-test	141	11,031
	Admin-train	405	18,122
	Admin-test	174	7911
	User-train	1349	19,318
	User-test	579	8339

roles based on pairs of keywords produces the highest accuracy for each data split with less than 50% accuracy for the 90/10 data split. The Technologist role has a noticeable increase in accuracy when evaluating frequency of IA based on the 70/30 data split. The 90/10 data split yields the least performance for each preliminary classification technique.

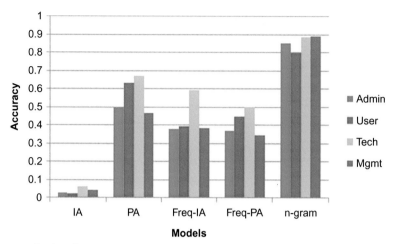

Fig. 8 Role classification based on 70/30 data split.

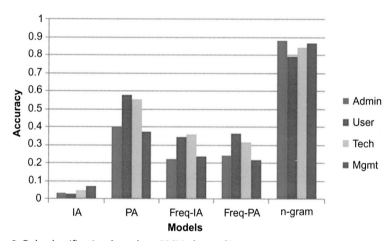

Fig. 9 Role classification based on 80/20 data split.

From this study, we show the accuracy of classifying users of organizational web-based systems based on four preliminary approaches and one SLM: *individual keywords, pairs of keywords, frequency of individual keywords, pairs of keywords, and n-grams*, using representative samples of data from pre-classified instances. Based on each data split and model, *n*-grams significantly outperform preliminary models with approximately 90% accuracy for many user roles. We hypothesize that the use of statistical language models could offer more predictive power for sequences of web-based interactions.

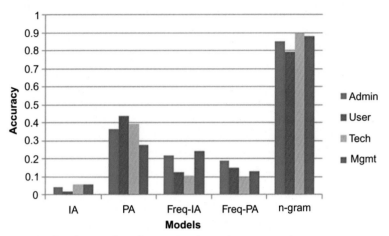

Fig. 10 Role classification based on 90/10 data split.

Table 4 Comparison of Natural Language and Web Behavior

Natural Language	Web Behavior Language	Example
Word	Link selection	View profile
Phrase	View	Watch online training video
Sentence	Action	Search for archived files
Paragraph	Activity	Register for course
Document	Event	Prepare course evaluation report

3.3 CUA Paradigm for Web-Based Applications

We now discuss key contributions of this work which serve as building blocks for the *Intruder Detector* tool.

3.3.1 Contribution 1: Model Selection

It is important to understand individual and role-based behavior to detect common patterns. Specifically, we would like to use web logs to build usage profiles for each user. Grammars can be defined for human behavior and natural language [52,53]. Table 4 illustrates the commonalities between natural language and web-based user behavior. Links or buttons in a web application represent a basic level of vocabulary for web behavior. A series of link clicks give the user the ability to *view* various portions of the website (e.g., course videos). Meaningful sequential link selections may lead to various *actions*, *activities*, or *events*. Since web logs represent sequential actions, they can be encoded as sequences of symbols and used with a standard NLP technique to build computational usage models [54]. In this work, we experiment with n-grams to model sequences of keywords, each of which represent a user action. We use n-grams, derived from Markov models, to understand similarity in user actions to classify the user's identity. These generative models can learn each category of users then classify the users based on the generated knowledge. This method gives us the ability to perform user authentication task with only positive training samples.

Classification of data becomes more feasible after n-grams have been derived. Let us illustrate how n-grams can be used for classification. Suppose a bigram model (i.e., $N = 2$) of user behavior that is captured after training is:

$$n = U_1 U_2 U_1 U_3 U_1 U_4 U_1 U_5 U_2 U_3,$$

where U_i is an observation from a user behavioral sequence. When a user's test sequence is read as $\{U_1, U_2, U_3\}$, bigrams are generated as $\{U_1 U_2, U_2 U_3\}$. The probability for this bigram to occur will be calculated using the following equation:

$$P = \frac{\# \text{ of valid observations}}{\# \text{of observations}} \tag{6}$$

The sequence is normal if P is greater than or equal to a preset threshold value, t. After applying Eq. (6) (i.e., $P = (2/2) = 1$) the observations will be identified as normal if we select a threshold value of 0.6. We assume user activity is largely based on role (i.e., access level). In our work, probabilities of n-grams are computed based on a large web log dataset (see Table 3). We assume users with the same role are likely to perform similar actions. System trust increases as the user interacts with the system and no outliers are identified in the CUA user model.

3.3.2 Contribution 2: Keyword Abstraction

Web server logs are obtained for system users and are grouped into sessions of activity by role. Access-level web-based systems have user roles already identified. An entry from the web server log is shown in Fig. 11. The format for web logs was standardized by the National Center for Supercomputing

134.164.78.20 - rleonard@HPCMP.HPC.MIL [08/April/2015:17:39:04 -0800] "GET /okc/admin_reg.jsp HTTP/1.0" 200 3401

Fig. 11 NCSA common log file format.

Table 5 NCSA Common Log File Entry

Field Name	Value	Description
Remote host address	134.164.78.20	IP address of client
Remote log name	—	Name is unavailable
User name	rleonard@HPCMP. HPC.MIL	User account that is accessing application
Date, time, and GMT offset	[08/April/ 2015:17:39:04- 0800]	Log file entry was created April 8, 2015 at 5:39 pm. The difference between the GMT and local time is 8 h
Request and protocol version	GET okc/admin reg_HTTP/1.0	GET command was used for the admin_reg file using HTTP version 1.0
Service status code	200	Request fulfilled successfully
Bytes sent	3401	Number of bytes sent

Applications (NCSA), founder of Mosaic browser, Apache HyperText Transfer Protocol (HTTP), and Common Gateway Interface (CGI). Table 5 describes the NCSA web log entry format.

We must preprocess the logs to remove unwanted entries. This helps validate the data captured in a user's session [55]. Preprocessing web log data can be difficult due to local caching and proxy servers. Web servers will not register repeated access to pages that are locally cached. If a proxy server is used, all web access entries will have the same identifier, even though different users are accessing the website. Therefore, preprocessing is a critical component of the usage behavioral process. The following steps are used for this process:

1. *Data Cleaning*: The process of data cleaning is very important to generate an accurate picture of user activity when navigating a web application. Removing irrelevant request, data fields/columns, and system generated text is essential. For web logs, various graphics and scripts are generated which add several entries to the log file. However, in the web AUE, only JavaServer Page (.jsp) entries show user behavior and are important for logging purposes. Therefore, all entries are removed that are not related to user activity.

2. *User Identification*: We use heuristics to determine users. A user is a person that interacts with the AUE. Once the data is clean, the remaining file

```
132.3.33.68 naboulsk@HPCMP.HPC.MIL - [22/Aug/2013:12:52:53 -0500] "GET /okc/html/cac_login.jsp HTTP/1.1" 443 200  744
132.3.33.68 naboulsk@HPCMP.HPC.MIL - [22/Aug/2013:12:53:47 -0500] "GET /okc/css/jquery.min.js HTTP/1.1" 443 200  57254
132.3.33.68 naboulsk@HPCMP.HPC.MIL - [22/Aug/2013:12:54:06 -0500] "GET /okc/wpmjsp/class_listing.jsp HTTP/1.1" 443 200  1
132.3.33.68 naboulsk@HPCMP.HPC.MIL - [22/Aug/2013:12:54:07 -0500] "GET /okc/wpmjsp/date-picker.js HTTP/1.1" 443 200  1677
132.3.33.68 naboulsk@HPCMP.HPC.MIL - [22/Aug/2013:12:54:07 -0500] "GET /okc/wpmjsp/courseviews.js HTTP/1.1" 443 200  2466
132.3.33.68 naboulsk@HPCMP.HPC.MIL - [22/Aug/2013:12:54:08 -0500] "GET /okc/prototype.js HTTP/1.1" 443 200  96311
132.3.33.68 naboulsk@HPCMP.HPC.MIL - [22/Aug/2013:12:54:08 -0500] "GET /okc/images/expandbutton-open.gif HTTP/1.1" 443 20
132.3.33.68 naboulsk@HPCMP.HPC.MIL - [22/Aug/2013:12:54:08 -0500] "GET /okc/wpmjsp/images/show-calendar.gif HTTP/1.1" 443
```

```
"GET_okc/html/cac_
"GET_okc/css/jquer
"GET_okc/wpmjsp/cl  "GET_okc/html/cac_
"GET_okc/wpmjsp/da  "GET_okc/css/jquer
"GET_okc/wpmjsp/cc  "GET_okc/wpmjsp/cl  "GET_okc/html/cac_
"GET_okc/prototype  "GET_okc/wpmjsp/da  "GET_okc/css/jquer
"GET_okc/images/ex  "GET_okc/wpmjsp/cc  "GET_okc/wpmjsp/cl
"GET_okc/wpmjsp/in  "GET_okc/prototype  "GET_okc/wpmjsp/da
"GET_okc/ContentAd  "GET_okc/images/ex  "GET_okc/wpmjsp/cc
"GET_okc/ContentAd  "GET_okc/wpmjsp/in  "GET_okc/prototype
"GET_okc/ContentAd  "GET_okc/ContentAd  "GET_okc/images/ex
"POST_/okc/Content  "GET_okc/ContentAd  "GET_okc/wpmjsp/in
"GET_okc/ContentAd  "GET_okc/ContentAd  "GET_okc/ContentAd
                    "POST_/okc/Content  "GET_okc/ContentAd
                    "GET_okc/ContentAd  "GET_okc/ContentAd
                                        "POST_/okc/Content
                                        "GET_okc/ContentAd
```

Fig. 12 Keyword generation.

entries are grouped by individual user. Each interaction in the web log file has a user-id association. Once the user-ids are captured, they are classified within *ID* based on their predefined role in the system. We avoid identifying users by IP address because the same IP address may be used by a group of users.

3. *Session Identification*: Session identification is used to divide user accesses into individual sessions [55]. User sessions are predefined in the AUE web log. After checking the database for the role of each user, sessions are then grouped by role.

4. *Keyword Generation*: For each relevant web log entry, a portion of the string is captured as a keyword. We load keywords for all users/roles into a database to build usage profiles. Fig. 12 shows an example of keywords extracted from a web log file. We do not consider parameters in this process because user entries would be too unique to categorize in a model.

3.3.3 Contribution 3: Tool Support

ID is a tool, created during this study, to abstract keywords from log files, build *n*-grams, and categorize users based on observed behavior. We use customized application programming interfaces (APIs), described in Section 3.4, to load input data and split the data based on predefined user roles or individual users. During the test phase of the experiments, a probability is assigned to a sequence of events. A probability alone does not provide continuous authentication. We use two approaches: binary and multiclass classification. Multiclass classification scores an input sequence according to one of many user models. For the mth classifier, the positive examples are all data points in class m and negative examples are all data points not in class m. Sequences of activity are categorized as belonging to the model which estimates the highest probability using the following equation:

$$u = \arg_m \max P(K, m) \qquad (7)$$

A more complex scheme which can also be useful for continuous authentication is binary classification [56,57]. For effective evaluation, this classification method requires more training and test data. This classification technique is used to judge a sequence as having likely been generated by a specific model (PASS) or not (FAIL). A probability threshold, t, is then used for this pass/fail type of judgment for a sequence. Any sequence whose probability exceeds this threshold should be considered as a PASS, $+1$, and otherwise considered FAIL, -1.

A decision rule is used to predict the class membership of a given sequence of behavioral keywords, K. When new samples are encountered, the following decision rule is used:

$$\begin{cases} P(K, m) > t, & \text{then} \quad y = +1 \\ P(K, m) < t, & \text{then} \quad y = -1 \end{cases}, \qquad (8)$$

where $P(K, m)$ is the probability the behavioral keyword sequence is generated by the mth user's n-gram model. The probabilities are estimated using a training set of labeled data

$$(m_0, y_0), (m_1, y_1), (m_2, y_2), \ldots, (m_n, y_n),$$

where label $y_i = \pm 1$ and depends on the class of m_i. Binary classification is used by a simple threshold and multiclass classification by comparing probabilities to translate n-gram models' estimations of sequence probability into decisions. The ability to make accurate classifications is investigated as supported by these algorithms.

3.3.4 Contribution 4: Evaluation Criteria

There is a large variation in the evaluation metrics used for classification systems. Metrics used for an analytical study must be appropriate for the problem domain. A confusion matrix, also known as contingency matrix, can be used to describe the performance of a classification system based on test data for which the positive (i.e., true) values are known. In Fig. 13, a confusion matrix is used for the classification of positive and negative examples. True positives, TP, represent cases in which the prediction and actual value are correct (i.e., positive). True negatives, TN, are captured when the actual and predicted value is negative. False negatives, FN, represent cases, where the prediction is negative and the actual category is positive. Finally, false positives, FP, capture cases, where the prediction is positive and the actual category is negative. False positives and false negatives are also known as *Type 1 errors* and *Type II errors*, respectively.

Optimal performance of any classification system is to reduce false positives and false negatives. Evaluation criteria, shown in Table 6, for a classifier can be obtained from statistical measures in Fig. 13. To efficiently evaluate these metrics, the dataset must be partitioned. We take a dataset whose class label we already know (i.e., actual data) and place them in a *training set*. To identify how well the classifier performs with unseen data, a *testing set* is used. This will indicate how well the classifier generalizes. In this case, both sets contain previously classified data.

We would also like these datasets to be large. Larger training sets provide better classifiers and larger test sets help build confidence in the evaluated metrics. We perform a repeated holdout method for the partition by randomly selecting instances for training and test sets. We use the 90/10, 80/20, and 70/30 training/test splits in this work. We repeat the hold

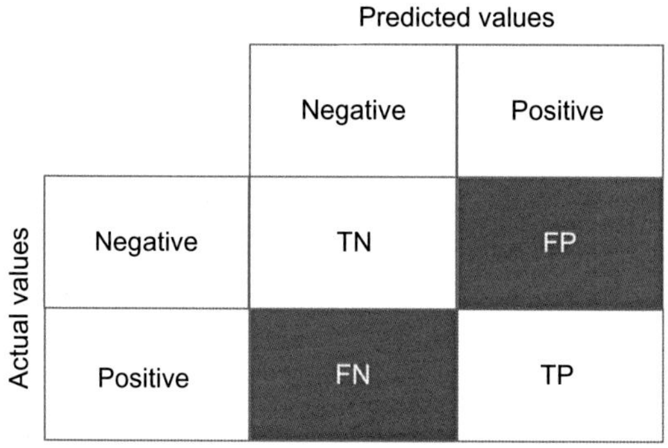

Predicted values

		Negative	Positive
Actual values	Negative	TN	FP
	Positive	FN	TP

Fig. 13 Confusion matrix.

Table 6 Metrics Computed From Confusion Matrix

Metric	Formula
Accuracy	$(TP + TN)/(TN + TP + FN + FP)$
Recall (true-positive rate)	$(TP)/(FN + TP)$
False-positive rate	$(FP)/(TN + FP)$
Specificity	$(TN)/(TN + FP)$ or 1 minus False-Positive Rate
Precision	$(TP)/(FP + TP)$
Prevalence	$(FN + TP)/(TN + TP + FN + FP)$
F-measure	$(2\ xPrecision\ xRecall)/(Precision + Recall)$

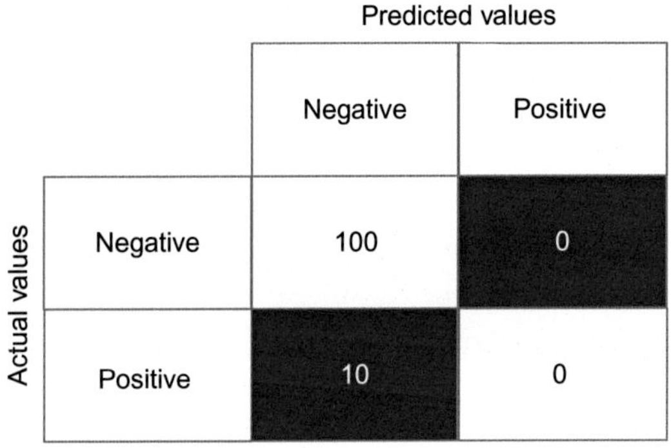

Predicted values

		Negative	Positive
Actual values	Negative	100	0
	Positive	10	0

Fig. 14 Confusion matrix example.

out method 10 times and average the results to get an overall value for the metric being observed.

Accuracy is the simplest form of evaluation and is used to determine how often the classifier is correct. If the classifier correctly labels half of the dataset, then we say its accuracy is 50%. In many cases, it seems obvious that we have better predictive power as the accuracy of a model increases. Suppose we have a binary classifier to detect the presence of breast cancer in patients. From Fig. 14, $accuracy = (0 + 100)/(10 + 0 + 100 + 0) = 90.9\%$. This model is completely useless with zero predictive power because the classifier is predicting only negative examples. However, the accuracy for this classifier is very high. This scenario represents an *Accuracy Paradox* which states that *models with a given level of accuracy may have greater predictive power than models with very high accuracy*. In some cases, accuracy alone can be misleading. This metric is better used together with other measures. Precision and recall address the imbalance that can occur in a dataset. Precision answers the following question: When the classifier predicts a positive example, how often is it correct? On the other hand, recall answers: When evaluating all the positive examples in a dataset, what fraction of the dataset did the classifier identify? A perfect classifier will have 100% precision and recall. However, in real world classification tasks, reaching this optimal performance is difficult to achieve. If the classifier is tweaked to offer very high recall, then precision rates suffer. Alternatively, classifiers that are tweaked for high precision rates suffer from poor recall rates. To provide balance, the F-measure is used as the weighted harmonic mean of precision and recall. There are many metrics for evaluating classification systems. In this work, we consider a specific set of metrics for evaluation since various metrics provide different and valuable insight into how each model performs. False-positive rates and prevalence are measured, in addition to, accuracy, recall, precision, and F-measure to provide additional analysis for each model.

3.4 Continuous User Authentication Infrastructure

We use several custom APIs for the continuous user authentication infrastructure. The WeblogDataHandler is a front-end API that is used to load keyword data and split it into training and test sets. Table 7 provides details for each method call. TestDataManager is a Java tool used for storing and retrieving keyword data (see Table 8). We use a nonrelational document database, MongoDB [e], as a back-end data store. MongoDB is a NoSql (i.e., nonrelational) database structured in favor of JavaScript Object Notation (JSON) documents. We serialize each keyword document into JSON before adding them to the MongoDB for storage.

We use the BerkeleyLM N-gram Language Model Library to construct n-gram models from keyword data. BerkeleyLM is a library for estimating and storing large n-gram language models in memory [58]. This library also provides efficient access to data. We extend this open source Java library with the TestDataManager and Analyzer APIs. Tables 9 and 10 show all methods used for these extensions.

Specifically, we use the categorizeStoredSequence method for multiclass classification and the acceptRawSequenceGivenModel method for binary classification. Each API is designed to handle large-scale experiments with

---

[e] http://www.mongodo.org.

Table 7 WeblogDataHandler: Front-End API for Training and Test Data Categorization

Method	Description
void splitLargeDataForScheme(String scheme)	Split abstracted keyword data
boolean categorizeSessions(String scheme, int modelOrder)	Categorize n-grams by role on the same data that trained models
boolean ngramsAgainstOthers(String scheme, String myGroup, int modelOrder, int ngramOrder, float threshold, boolean mine)	Returns n-gram categories when using training and test data from various groups
float categorizeStrings(String scheme, int modelOrder, List < String > stringstoCategorize, List < String > actualGroups, String method, float threshold, String modelChoice)	Returns the n-gram probability based on the binary or multiclass categorization method

Table 8 TestDataManager API: Storing and Retrieving Keyword Data

Method	Description
boolean clearTestSuite(String dbId, String suiteId)	Clear the suite before saving new keywords
boolean addArtifactToTest(String dbId, String testId, String artifactPath, ArtifactProcessor)	Save the keyword file for each user/role to the database
boolean addTestToSuite(String dbId, String testId, String suiteId)	Add keywords with a given ID to a suite with given ID

Table 9 Analyzer API: Intermediate n-gram Model Computation

Method	Description
String categorizeStoredSequence(String test, List < String > suiteId, int order ArtifactProcessor processorClass, boolean useWrapperSymbols)	Categorizes stored sequence for multiclassification approach
String acceptRawSequenceGivenModel(String test, List < String > suiteId, int order ArtifactProcessor processorClass, boolean useWrapperSymbols, float threshold)	Categorizes stored sequence for binary classification approach using threshold value

Table 10 TestDataManager API: n-gram Models

Method	Description
ArrayEncodedProbBackoffLm < String > computeModel(String dbId, String suiteId, int maxOrder)	Compute an n-gram model from a given test suite with a given order, returning the result as a BerkeleyLM object
ArrayEncodedProbBackoffLm < String > getNgramModel(String dbId, String suiteId)	Return the n-gram model currently associated with a test suite

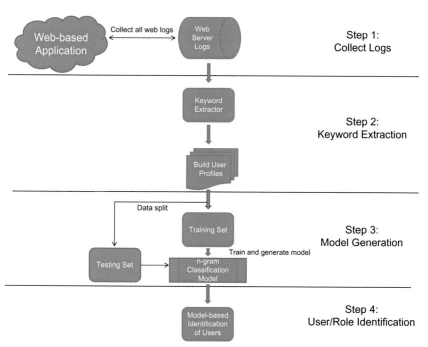

Fig. 15 CUA framework description.

keyword data. Fig. 15 provides a detailed high-level view of the CUA framework. This figure outlines the steps we follow to complete this task.

3.5 Intruder Detector in Action

We will now show, via an example, how *ID* works when web log data is present. Assume that, over time, web logs have been collected for users

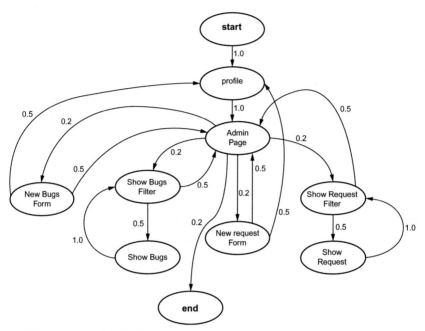

Fig. 16 *n*-gram model of Alice.

of a web-based system. *ID* has developed, for each user, an *n*-gram model, essentially representing the user's typical behavior. Alice, an administrator, typically starts from her user profile page to connect to the admin page. From the admin page, she can perform a set of tasks associated with this role, namely, submit new bugs, view existing bugs, submit new change requests, view current change requests, etc.

Fig. 16 represents an *n*-gram behavioral user model for Alice. The nodes in the model represent actions that Alice performs on the web pages. Edges represent a workflow relationship between these actions; the numeric values represent the probability that these actions will occur. For example, a probability of 1.0 from "start" to "profile" implies that Alice always starts at the "profile" page; once in the "admin" page, the user is likely to start a "new bug form" with the probability of 0.2. Once in the "new bug form," Alice has the option to go back to the "profile page" or "admin page" (with equal probability); the user may then return to the "new bug form." However, there is no option to go directly to the "show bugs filter" page from a "new bug form."

ID has a stored model for Alice since she has used the web application in the past. However, *ID* is continuously monitoring her. As she interacts with the software, a series of web requests, in the form of web log entries, are recognized by the tool. These web log entries are translated into a sequence of keywords: (*start, profile, admin page, show bugs filter, show bugs, show bugs filter, admin page, end*). *ID* continuously checks all the stored models and matches the sequence to Alice's model. Alice is authenticated and allowed to continue using the application.

After some time, Alice decides to take a break and walks away from her computer before logging out of the system. Bob, without authorization, takes control of her session. Bob is a user with lower system privileges and has no idea how to work the system as an Admin. The keywords generated from Bob's interactions are (*admin page, show request filter, admin page, new bug form, admin page, end*). When comparing this sequence to the usage profile for Alice, *ID* identifies Bob as a potential intruder and the session is ended (or Bob is asked to reauthenticate, depending on how *ID* is configured).

There are several points to note regarding this overview scenario. First, we deliberately keep the *n*-gram model very simple so as to be easily understandable. This simple model represents $N = 2$ with a history of zero. At this step, it is important to understand that the *n*-gram model captures much more information than is apparent with this simple example. Second, we show only one model (e.g., Alice's model). In general, *ID* will maintain multiple models, one for each user. Having a model for Bob may give *ID* the ability to capture his identity. However, there are some limitations to pinpointing Bob's identity which will be discussed in this work. Third, such models may be maintained for classes of users, not just individual users. It is important to distinguish between multiple user types and their different behaviors (e.g., admin users typically access the "take tape backups" page; conventional users do not).

Finally, *ID* can be configured to incrementally improve its models during execution. Consider that Alice executes a new sequence of actions not contained in her *n*-gram model. *ID* will recognize the mismatch and ask for reauthentication (e.g., via a password or supervisor approval). If this transaction is successful, then the sequence of actions that was not recognized is added to the *n*-gram model, thereby improving its accuracy. This will also be the case if the user interface is updated. Subsequently, if Alice performs the same sequence of actions, *ID* will recognize it as legitimately belonging to Alice. When fielded, we envision *ID* to be used in a training mode to build baseline models of all users, and then used in a deployment mode.

4. CONCLUSIONS

Many organizations are becoming increasingly aware of their security posture. It is important to identify cybersecurity-related risks and develop strategies to mitigate them. Continuous user authentication is one approach that can be utilized to identify impersonations and misappropriation of authentication credentials [59]. Specifically, this technique can be used with web applications to provide reliable and secure authentication. In this work, we present challenges that occur when modeling the behavior of users that interact with web-based software. We then present an approach to address the need for web-based continuous user authentication.

We obtain less than optimal results when conducting a feasibility study, using a real world application, to assess the need for our approach. After exploring various statistical language models, we employ the use of n-grams to capture user interaction with web-based software. We use n-grams to model sequences and subsequences of user actions, their orderings, and the temporal relationships that make them unique. After learning the behavior, we illustrate the ability to classify the models using multiclass classification to identify role and/or individual user characteristics. Results show model-specific differences in user behavior with performance highly dependent on session and keyword size. We identify outliers in variable length keyword sequences using the binary classification technique. Results from this approach show the rate at which each model rejects uncharacteristic sequences and accepts valid sequences. Our CUA implementation is continual, nonintrusive, and behavioral.

In summary, the contributions of this work include the following:

- We develop a novel keyword abstraction technique to preprocess large volumes of web logs. This method helps reduce incomplete, noisy, and inconsistent data.
- We explore various statistical language models to capture the behavior of users as they interact with web-based organizational information systems.
- We develop a continuous user authentication framework, based on n-grams, to classify user sessions into roles and individual usage profiles. We also use this approach to identify outliers in role-based user behavior.
- We introduce a set of evaluation metrics to test the feasibility of our approach.

4.1 Future Work

Our work in continuous user authentication is a foundational approach for web-based user behavioral analysis. There are various ways our work can be extended to explore this field of study. We conclude that with two of the four role-based models considered, the correct identification of negative samples was above 90% as well as a 100% correct acceptance of positive samples. These findings are promising and motivate future work to better understand model-specific differences which make this task more difficult for some cases (e.g., Admin and Technologist roles) than others. In particular, the finding that User sessions can so easily be protected against uncharacteristic usage is promising.

Many web applications have different sensitivity levels for security threats. Some systems must be protected at higher levels than other systems. There is a need to investigate an adaptive scheme (i.e., tunable parameter) to determine thresholds for different applications. The thresholds may be adjusted based on a user's role, application infrastructure, business logic, usage patterns, etc.

In many settings, statistical language models are computationally intensive. Building n-grams over large datasets pose challenges to memory and speed [60]. The computational cost of running these models should be calculated in real time to access the current usability performance. There may be a need to utilize a HPC environment to increase prediction time in an effort to help prevent or interrupt malicious web use. It will be useful to explore parallelization on various platforms such as shared memory processor machines and Linux clusters with a high-speed network. Instead of starting with a parallel programming framework such as MPI or OpenMP, many standard tools exist. Parallelization scripts from the IRST Language Modeling Toolkit are an acceptable starting point to distribute tasks to a cluster of machines [61].

There are various performance metrics available for classification tasks. The performance metrics used in this work can be extended to include the time it takes to identify legitimate and malicious use. When outliers are identified, it is important to detect this activity before the active session is complete. However, in some cases, this time metric may allow some flexibility to help application forensics analyst gather reliable evidence to use against perpetrators.

A combination of machine learning techniques for classification should be explored for continuous user authentication. In this work, we use supervised learning techniques to access the classification of user behavior. Exploring how semisupervised and unsupervised learning help make data-driven predictions or decisions is an open area of research in this domain.

Finally, our work uses a single modality for CUA tasks. The use of a multimodal approach may prove to provide a more transparent authentication process and help reduce false-positive rates. Even though our models are able to detect legitimate users and outliers, the false alarms can be annoying and decrease usability dramatically. For example, a combination of web logs, database logs, and graphical user interface (GUI) accesses can be used to obtain more information about a user's behavior. Keyboard and mouse interactions may also be integrated to provide a cost-effective solution for continuous authentication. At any time, when one modality is not available, another one is able to capture such behavior and provide a highly predictive system.

In summary, we have shown how sequences and subsequences of user interactions are captured within statistical language models to continuously identify users, user types, and outliers in user behavior. To provide focus, we have limited our work to web-based organizational information systems. However, the CUA domain can be extended to context-aware computing, Internet of Things, and people-centric applications.

REFERENCES

[1] Richard P. Guidorizzi, Security: active authentication, IT Professional 15 (4) (2013) 4–7.
[2] SplashData. Splashdata news, 2015 (Online; accessed 03 October 2015).
[3] Koichiro Niinuma, Anil K. Jain, Continuous user authentication using temporal information. Proc. SPIE 7667, Biometric Technology for Human Identification VII, 76670L (April 14, 2010). http://dx.doi.org/10.1117/12.847886.
[4] Animesh Patcha, Jung-Min Park, An overview of anomaly detection techniques: existing solutions and latest technological trends, Comput. Netw. 51 (12) (2007) 3448–3470.
[5] Koichiro Niinuma, Unsang Park, Anil K. Jain, Soft biometric traits for continuous user authentication, IEEE Trans. Inf. Forensics Secur. 5 (4) (2010) 771–780.
[6] DARPA. Active authentication. http://www.darpa.mil/program/active authentication, 2013 (Online; accessed 24 November 2015).
[7] Chao Shen, Zhongmin Cai, Xiaohong Guan, Continuous authentication for mouse dynamics: a pattern-growth approach, in: Proceedings of the 2012 42nd Annual IEEE/IFIP International Conference on Dependable Systems and Networks (DSN), DSN'12, IEEE Computer Society, Washington, DC, 2012, pp. 1–12.
[8] Fabian Monrose, Aviel D. Rubin, Keystroke dynamics as a biometric for authentication, Future Gener. Comput. Syst. 16 (4) (2000) 351–359.
[9] Information System. Information system, 2015 (Online; accessed 03 October 2015).
[10] Leslie Milton, Bryan Robbins, Atif Memon, N-gram based user behavioral model for continuous user authentication, in: The Proceedings of the Eighth International

Conference on Emerging Security Information, Systems, and Technologies (SECURWARE 2014), 2014.

[11] Daniel Jurafsky, James Martin, Speech and Language Processing: An Introduction to Natural Language Processing, Computational Linguistics, and Speech Recognition, second ed., Pearson Prentice Hall, Englewood Cliffs, NJ, 2009.

[12] Yubico. Yubico. http://www.yubico.com/, 2013 (Online; accessed 1 November 2013).

[13] Dino Schweitzer, Jeff Boleng, Colin Hughes, Louis Murphy, Visualizing keyboard pattern passwords, Inf. Vis. 10 (2) (2011) 127–133.

[14] Andrew J. Klosterman, Gregory R. Ganger, Secure Continuous Biometric-Enhanced Authentication: Technical report, Carnegie Mellon University, Pittsburgh, PA, 2000.

[15] Michael Kaminsky, George Savvides, David Mazieres, M. Frans Kaashoek, Decentralized user authentication in a global file system, in: Proceedings of the Nineteenth ACM Symposium on Operating Systems Principles, SOSP'03, ACM, New York, NY, 2003, pp. 60–73.

[16] Richard Chow, Markus Jakobsson, Ryusuke Masuoka, Jesus Molina, Yuan Niu, Elaine Shi, Zhexuan Song, Authentication in the clouds: a framework and its application to mobile users, in: Proceedings of the 2010 ACM Workshop on Cloud Computing Security Workshop, CCSW'10, ACM, New York, NY, 2010, pp. 1–6.

[17] The Wall Street Journal. U.S. suspects hackers in china breached about 4 million people's records, officials say. http://www.wsj.com/articles/u-s-suspects-hackers-in-china-behind-government-data-breach-sources-say-1433451888, 2015 (Online; accessed 17 November 2015).

[18] Eric Grosse, Mayank Upadhyay, Authentication at scale, IEEE Secur. Priv. 11 (2013) 15–22.

[19] I. Deutschmann, P. Nordstrom, L. Nilsson, Continuous authentication using behavioral biometrics, IT Professional 15 (4) (2013) 12–15.

[20] Harini Jagadeesan, Michael S. Hsiao, Continuous authentication in computers, Continuous Authentication Using Biometrics: Data, Models, and Metrics, vol. 1, Information Science Reference (an imprint of IGI Global), Hershey, PA, 2012, pp. 40–66.

[21] Alphan Altinok, Matthew Turk, Temporal integration for continuous multimodal biometrics, in: Proceedings in Workshop on Multimodal User Authentication. Santa Barbara, CA, 2003, pp. 131–137.

[22] Hang-Bong Kang, Myung-Ho Ju, Multi-modal feature integration for secure authentication, in: Proceedings of the 2006 International Conference on Intelligent Computing, ICIC'06, vol. Part I, Springer-Verlag, Berlin, Heidelberg, 2006, pp. 1191–1200.

[23] Yinglian Xie, Fang Yu, Qifa Ke, Martin Abadi, Eliot Gillum, Krish Vitaldevaria, Jason Walter, Junxian Huang, Zhuoqing Morley Mao, Innocent by association: early recognition of legitimate users, in: Proceedings of the 2012 ACM Conference on Computer and Communications Security, CCS'12, ACM, New York, NY, 2012, pp. 353–364.

[24] Pang Wu, Joy Zhang, Jiang Zhu, Xiao Wang, SenSec: mobile security through passive sensing, in: Proceedings of the 2013 International Conference on Computing, Networking and Communications (ICNC), ICNC'13, IEEE Computer Society, Washington, DC, 2013, pp. 1128–1133.

[25] Hataichanok Saevanee, Nathan Clarke, Steven Furnell, Valerio Biscione, Continuous user authentication using multi-modal biometrics, Comput. Secur. 53 (2015) 234–246.

[26] Tee Kiah Chia, Khe Chai Sim, Haizhou Li, Hwee Tou Ng, Statistical lattice-based spoken document retrieval, ACM Trans. Inf. Syst. 28 (1) (2010). 2:1–2:30.

[27] Jay M. Ponte, W. Bruce Croft, A language modeling approach to information retrieval, in: Proceedings of the 21st Annual International ACM SIGIR Conference on Research and Development in Information Retrieval, SIGIR'98, ACM, New York, NY, 1998, pp. 275–281.

[28] Deyi Xiong, Min Zhang, Haizhou Li, Enhancing language models in statistical machine translation with backward n-grams and mutual information triggers, in: Proceedings of the 49th Annual Meeting of the Association for Computational Linguistics: Human Language Technologies, HLT'11, vol. 1, Association for Computational Linguistics, Stroudsburg, PA, 2011, pp. 1288–1297.

[29] Michael Collins, Brian Roark, Murat Saraclar, Discriminative syntactic language modeling for speech recognition, in: Proceedings of the 43rd Annual Meeting on Association for Computational Linguistics, ACL'05, Association for Computational Linguistics, Stroudsburg, PA., 2005, pp. 507–514.

[30] Ronald Rosenfeld, Two decades of statistical language modeling: where do we go from here, in: Proceedings of the IEEE, 2000, p. 2000.

[31] M. Egmont-Petersen, D. de Ridder, H. Handels, Image processing with neural networks—a review, Pattern Recogn. 35 (10) (2002) 2279–2301.

[32] Adam Fadlalla, Chien-Hua Lin, An analysis of the applications of neural networks in finance, Interfaces 31 (4) (2001) 112–122.

[33] MariaGraa Ruano, AntnioE Ruano, On the use of artificial neural networks for biomedical applications, in: Valentina Emilia Balas, Jnos Fodor, Annamria R. Vrkonyi-Kczy, Joszef Dombi, Lakhmi C. Jain (Eds.), Soft Computing Applications Advances in Intelligent Systems and Computing, vol. 195, Springer, Berlin Heidelberg, 2013, pp. 433–451.

[34] H. Larochelle, Y. Bengio, J. Louradour, P. Lamblin, Exploring strategies for training deep neural networks, J. Mach. Learn. Res. 10 (2009) 1–40.

[35] Rajendra Akerkar, Priti Sajja, Knowledge-Based Systems, first ed., Jones and Bartlett Publishers, Inc., USA, 2009.

[36] Tomáš Mikolov, Anoop Deoras, Daniel Povey, Lukáš Burget, Jan Černocký, Strategies for training large scale neural network language models, in: Proceedings of ASRU 2011, IEEE Signal Processing Society, Olomouc, Czech Republic, 2011, pp. 196–201.

[37] Adam L. Berger, Vincent J. Della Pietra, Stephen A. Della Pietra, A maximum entropy approach to natural language processing, Comput. Linguist. 22 (1) (1996) 39–71.

[38] Ronald Rosenfeld, A maximum entropy approach to adaptive statistical language modeling, Comput. Speech Lang. 10 (1996) 187–228.

[39] Lalit R. Bahl, Peter F. Brown, Peter V. de Souza, Robert L. Mercer, Readings in speech recognition, Tree-based statistical language model for natural language speech recognition, Morgan Kaufmann Publishers Inc., San Francisco, CA., 1990, pp. 507–514. Chapter A.

[40] Varun Chandola, Arindam Banerjee, Vipin Kumar, Anomaly detection: a survey, ACM Comput. Surv. 41 (3) (2009) 15:1–15:58.

[41] Leonard A. Breslow, David W. Aha, Simplifying decision trees: a survey, Knowl. Eng. Rev. 12 (1) (1997) 1–40.

[42] Mikhail Petrovskiy, A data mining approach to learning probabilistic user behavior models from database access log, in: Joaquim Filipe, Boris Shishkov, Markus Helfert (Eds.), Software and data technologies, volume 10 of communications in computer and information science, Springer, Berlin Heidelberg, 2008, pp. 323–332.

[43] C.E. Shannon, A mathematical theory of communication, SIGMOBILE Mob. Comput. Commun. Rev. 5 (1) (2001) 3–55.

[44] Mukund Deshpande, George Karypis, Selective markov models for predicting web page accesses, ACM Trans. Internet Technol. 4 (2) (2004) 163–184.

[45] Eren Manavoglu, Dmitry Pavlov, C. Lee Giles, Probabilistic user behavior models, in: Proceedings of the Third IEEE International Conference on Data Mining, ICDM'03, IEEE Computer Society, Washington, DC., 2003, p. 203.

[46] Leonard E. Baum, Ted Petrie, Statistical inference for probabilistic functions of finite state markov chains, Ann. Math. Statist. 37 (6) (1966) 1554–1563.

[47] Leonard E. Baum, J.A. Eagon, An inequality with applications to statistical estimation for probabilistic functions of markov processes and to a model for ecology, Bull. Amer. Math. Soc. 73 (3) (1967) 360–363.

[48] Leonard E. Baum, T. Petrie, G. Soules, N. Weiss, Maximization technique occurring in the statistical analysis of probabilistic functions of markov chains, Ann. Math. Stat. 41 (6) (1970) 360–363.

[49] L. Rabiner, A tutorial on hidden markov models and selected applications in speech recognition, Proc. IEEE 77 (2) (1989) 257–286.

[50] L. Razmerita, An ontology-based framework for modeling user behavior—a case study in knowledge management, IEEE Trans. Syst. Man Cybern. Part A Syst. Hum., IEEE Transactions on 41 (4) (2011) 772–783.

[51] CAC. Dod common access card. http://www.cac.mill/, 2015 (Online; accessed 11 September 2015).

[52] James V. Wertsch, Mind as Action, Oxford University Press, Oxford, England, 1998.

[53] Kenneth Burke, Language as Symbolic Action, University of California Press, Berkeley, CA, 1966.

[54] Jimmy Lin, W. John Wilbur, Modeling actions of pubmed users with n-gram language models, Inf. Retr. 12 (4) (2009) 487–503.

[55] Robert Cooley, Bamshad Mobasher, Jaideep Srivastava, Data preparation for mining world wide web browsing patterns, Knowl. Inf. Syst. 1 (1999) 5–32.

[56] Yiguang Liu, Zhisheng You, Liping Cao, A novel and quick svm-based multi-class classifier, Pattern Recogn. 39 (11) (2006) 2258–2264.

[57] Paul Honeine, Zineb Noumir, Cdric Richard, Multiclass classification machines with the complexity of a single binary classifier, Signal Process. 93 (5) (2013) 1013–1026.

[58] Adam Pauls, Dan Klein, Faster and smaller n-gram language models, in: Proceedings of the 49th Annual Meeting of the Association for Computational Linguistics: Human Language Technologies HLT'11, vol. 1, Association for Computational Linguistics, Stroudsburg, PA, 2011, pp. 258–267.

[59] Introduction to Continuous Authentication, IT Policy and Ethics: Concepts, Methodologies, Tools, and Applications. IGI Global, Hershey, PA, 2013, pp. 1–21. Web. 16 Jan. 2017. http://dx.doi.org/10.4018/978-1-4666-2919-6.ch001.

[60] Lars Bungum, Bjorn Gamback, Efficient n-gram language modeling for billion word web corpora, in: Workshop on Challenges in the Management of Large Corpora, LREC'12, 2012.

[61] M. Federico, N. Bertoldi, M. Cettolo, IRSTLM: an open source toolkit for handling large scale language models, in: Proceedings of Interspeech, 2008.

ABOUT THE AUTHOR

Dr. Leslie C. Leonard is a Computer Scientist with the Information Technology Laboratory at the U.S. Army Engineer Research and Development Center (ERDC) in Vicksburg, Mississippi. She currently serves as the Cybersecurity Research Lead for the High Performance Computing Modernization Program (HPCMP). The HPCMP is a technology-led, innovation-focused program committed to extending high performance computing (HPC) to address the Department of Defense's (DoD's) most significant challenges for the research, development, test, and evaluation (RDT&E) community.

Dr. Leonard began her career with ERDC in 2005 as a software developer. She has participated on several interdisciplinary teams of computer scientists, computer engineers, and civil engineers in large-scale research and software development projects.

Dr. Leonard received her Bachelor of Science and Master of Science degrees in Computer Science from Jackson State University in 2004 and 2008, respectively. She received her Doctor of Philosophy degree in Computer Science from the University of Maryland, College Park in December 2015.

Dr. Leonard has received several honors and awards during her career. She was awarded the Modern Day Technology Leadership award at the 2009 Black Engineer of the Year Awards STEM Global Competitive Conference. In addition, she was identified as an Emerging Leader at the 2008 U.S. Army Corps of Engineers (USACE) Emerging Leaders Conference and served as a Team Leader during the 2009 USACE Emerging Leaders Conference. She has also received the Department of the Army Commander's Award, Achievement Medal for Civilian Service, and the USACE Command Sergeant Major Award for Excellence.

## CHAPTER TWO

Advances in Model-Based Testing of GUI-Based Software

I. Banerjee
University of Maryland, College Park, MD, United States

Contents

Abstract

The Graphical User Interface (GUI) is an integral component of contemporary computer software. A stable and reliable GUI is necessary for correct functioning of software applications. Comprehensive verification of the GUI is a routine part of most software development life cycles. The input space of a GUI is typically large, making exhaustive verification difficult. GUI defects are often revealed by exercising parts of the GUI that interact with each other.

Advances in Computers, Volume 105
ISSN 0065-2458
http://dx.doi.org/10.1016/bs.adcom.2016.12.003

In recent years, *model-based* methods, which target specific GUI interactions, have been developed. These methods create a formal model of the GUI's input space from *specification* of the GUI, *visible GUI behaviors* and *static analysis* of the GUI's program code, and *dynamic analysis* of interactions between the GUI and its program code.

This chapter discusses recent advances in testing GUI-based software. It describes techniques that generate testcases for GUI-based applications. Some popular methods are described, specifically ones that create a model of the GUI and generate testcases based on the GUI model.

1. INTRODUCTION

Computer software provides various methods for users to interact with the software. A popular method for interacting with computer software is via the graphical user interfaces (GUI). A GUI-based software system (GUI-based software or GUI-based application) is one that provides a GUI as a method of interacting with it. They belong to the larger class of *Event-Driven* [1] software systems.

The GUI of GUI-based software presents a visual interface, by means of a visual display system. A user of the software can execute actions, using an appropriate input device (such as mouse, keyboard, or touch) on the GUI.

Testing a GUI-based application consists of many steps. It includes creating a deterministic test environment, identifying testcases, executing the testcases, and determining if the testcase revealed a software defect. This chapter describes techniques for creating testcases for testing the GUI of a GUI-based application. Some GUI testing terms that will be used here are defined as follows:

widget: A GUI *widget* is a primitive element of the GUI. Many GUI widgets together constitute the GUI of a GUI-based application. For example, the *'Save'* and *'Cancel'* buttons in the *'Save As…'* dialog box of Microsoft Notepad are widgets. The layout of GUI widgets is often hierarchical, where a GUI *container* (such as the *'Save As…'* dialog box) contains a set of primitive GUI widgets or other GUI containers.

event: A GUI *event* is an instance of executing an action (e.g., *click*, *select*) by the user on a *widget* (e.g., *'Save'*, *Checkbox*).

event sequence: An ordered set of GUI events is an *event sequence*. An event sequence can be executed on the GUI by the user or by a software agent such as a GUI testing tool. As an example, *'File'* → *'Save As…'* → *'Save'* is an event sequence that can be executed on Microsoft Notepad immediately after it has been launched.

testcase: A GUI event sequence that can be executed on a GUI-based application is a *testcase*. A testcase is typically executed on the application at a time when the application's GUI state is known, for example, immediately after the application is launched.

length-*n* testcase: A GUI testcase containing *n* *consecutive* GUI events of *interest*, is a *length-n* *testcase*. A length-*n* testcase may be prefixed with additional GUI events that make it possible to execute the first event in the length-n testcase. For example, *'Paste'* → *'Edit'* → *'Select All'* is a length-3 testcase in Microsoft Notepad. However, this may be prefixed with the event *'Edit'* to reach the *'Paste'* event, after the application is launched. Similarly events may be inserted between the events of interest in a length-n testcase so that an event of interest can be reached from the preceding event of interest.

The terms *event* and *widget* may be interchanged, when the context is clear. For example, a statement 'the *Save* event was executed' would expand to 'the *click* event was executed on the *Save* button widget'.

1.1 GUI Testing Challenges

Functional verification of the GUI of GUI-based applications has always been an important part of their development life cycle. This verification does not focus on the underlying 'business-logic' of the application, although defects in that part of the software may also be revealed. As with other software components, verification of the GUI has its own unique set of challenges.

Verification of the GUI typically entails execution of a selected set of testcases on the GUI of the application and comparing the resulting state of the GUI with an *expected* state (using an *oracle* [2]). Given a GUI, with hundreds or thousands of events, the possible number of input event sequences can be very large, potentially infinite (for example, a user can execute *'Edit'* → *'Paste'* repeatedly on Microsoft Notepad). Hence, it becomes challenging to (1) identify the complete set of executable testcases, (2) prioritize the testcases in a suitable order, (3) execute testcases, manually or automatically, within a reasonable time, and (4) verify that execution of the testcase produced the expected results.

In *manual verification*, a human tester typically (1) launches the application, (2) identifies a testcase, (3) clicks on widgets following the prescribed order of the testcase, and (4) repeats steps 2–3 or 1–3 until a testing criteria has been achieved. When this method is employed for testing the application, it becomes challenging for the tester to (1) identify all testcases, (2) prioritize and select testcases according to some criteria, (3) execute the selected testcases without error or omission, and (4) verify the result of executing each testcase.

Automated verification also has similar challenges. *Capture/Replay* (record/replay) [3] is a popular method for automated verification of the GUI. In this method, a human tester first executes a set of testcases, on the GUI, that is observed and *captured* by the *capture tool*. At a later time, the *replay tool* executes the same testcases on the GUI to detect potential regressions. Using this method, however, the human tester may still miss out 'important' testcases. Besides capture/replay, exhaustive execution of all possible test-cases, in an automated manner, is typically impractical, owing to the large number of testcases and limited time allocated for the verification process.

In the last decade, *Model-based* testing [4–11] has been adopted as a pop-ular method for GUI testing. Some of the model-based methods have pro-duced practical methods for (1) reverse engineering the GUI of a GUI-based software to extract its structure, (2) creating a semantic model of the GUI such as EFG [9], EIG [7] from the extracted structure, and (3) creating 'important' testcases based on the semantic models. Model-based testing addresses the challenges of creating good GUI testcases.

1.2 Radio Button Demo

A simple Java application, shown in Fig. 1, called `Radio Button Demo` will be used as a running example. Different GUI models for this application will be constructed and explained. The application has one *top-level window*, `Radio Button Demo`, and one *modal window*, `Exit Confirmation`, which is invoked by clicking the `Exit` button. Widgets of interest on the application are labeled w_0 through w_8. A GUI event can be executed on all these widgets except for w_4, which can only display GUI content.

The next section describes a set of methods that create GUI testcases.

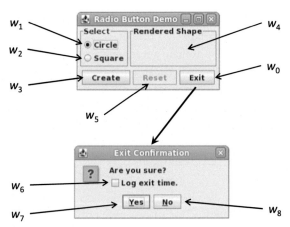

Fig. 1 A Java application, `Radio Button Demo`. It has one top-level window, `Radio Button Demo`, and one modal window, `Exit Confirmation`, that is opened by the `Exit` button. Nine relevant widgets are labeled w_0 to w_8.

2. METHODS

Verification of the GUI of GUI-based application has been performed using different methods. Popular techniques that have been attempted are
1. Capture and replay-based
2. Model-based

Capture and replay methods consist of two phases. In the first phase testcases are identified by the human tester. Different methods have been developed for identifying a testcase, such as recording the display coordinates of GUI events and using display content to identify the location of GUI events. In the second phase, the recorded testcase is replayed (executed) on the application. Changes, if any, in the application's GUI are noted during the replay phase and are analyzed to determine if they reveal a defect. Table 1 lists the capture/replay techniques that are described in this section.

Model-based GUI testing can also be broadly partitioned into two distinct phases. In the first phase, a *model* of the GUI is created. Creating the model may be *automated* or *manual* or a combination of both. In the second phase, testcases are created (manually or automatically) based on the model. Most model-based GUI testing techniques are concerned with developing modeling techniques that detect more defects with fewer number of testcases. Table 2 lists the GUI models discussed in this chapter and the family of modeling techniques it belongs to. From this table the Event–Code Interaction model is discussed in Section 3. This remaining models are described in this section.

2.1 Standard Capture/Replay

Capture and replay is a commonly used method for testing the GUI of a GUI-based application. A traditional capture/replay tool consists of the *capture* tool and the *replay* tool. In the first phase of testing a GUI-based application, the tester first identifies a sequence of GUI events as a testcase. The application and the capture tool are then started. The tester proceeds to

Table 1 Capture/Replay Methods for Testing the GUI of a GUI-Based Application

Family	Method/Model	Sections
Capture and replay	Standard	Section 2.1
	Image recognition	Section 2.2

It requires the assistance of a human tester to identify and create testcases.

Table 2 Model-Based Methods for Modeling the GUI of a GUI-Based Application

Family	Model	Sections
State machine	Finite state machine	Section 2.3
	Variable finite state machine	Section 2.4
	Complete interaction sequence	Section 2.5
	Faulty complete interaction sequence	Section 2.6
Workflow	Event-Flow Graph	Section 2.7
	Event-Interaction Graph	Section 2.8
	Event-Semantic Interaction Graph	Section 2.9
Event sequence	AI planning	Section 2.10
	Genetic algorithm	Section 2.11
Combinatorial	Coverage arrays	Section 2.12
Program code	Event–Code Interaction Graph	Section 3

Testcases are created using the model.

manually execute the GUI events on the application. The capture tool observes the execution and records properties of the GUI events executed by the tester. In particular the capture tool records the screen coordinates where mouse clicks were executed. It also records keyboard inputs received by the application. The recorded properties of the testcase are stored by the capture tool as a testcase.

Fig. 2 shows the creation of a GUI testcase using a traditional capture/ replay tool. The tester has identified a testcase, say T, as the sequence of events square $\rightarrow$ create $\rightarrow$ exit $\rightarrow$ yes. In Fig. 2A the tester launches the Radio Button Demo application and executes this testcase. A capture tool executing on the computer observes and records the screen coordinates of the mouse clicks. In this figure the screen coordinates are shown using colored $\star$ symbols. The GUI testcase, T, stored by the capture tool is a set of screen coordinates. Here $T = (100, 200), (100, 300), (300, 300), (900, 300)$. Fig. 2B shows the recorded testcase T.

During the second phase of testing, the replay tool will execute a recorded testcase on the application. The replay tool launches the application and retrieves a testcase, say T. It then executes the recorded GUI events on the application by mimicking the tester's actions. The replayer will essentially perform the sequence of events described in Fig. 2A. A testcase is

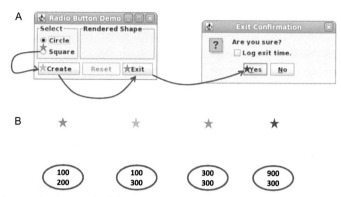

Fig. 2 Capture/replay method for creating a GUI testcase for the Radio Button Demo application. (A) The tester identifies and executes a testcase on the application. (B) The *capture* tool creates a testcase as a set of screen coordinates where GUI events are executed by the tester.

determined to have revealed a defect if the application crashes while replaying a testcase. Other methods for detecting a software defect may be implemented by the replay tool, such as comparing parts of the screen during the replay phase with the screen contents captured during the capture phase.

A drawback of the traditional capture/replay technique is that the location of GUI widgets may change between two invocations of the application or when the execution environment changes. It may also change during the development of the application, for example, between the Alpha and Beta versions of the application. Such changes may cause the replay tool to execute GUI events on incorrect locations of the application. This drawback is because the capture tool records the screen coordinates of GUI events without recording semantic information about the event or the widget.

Robust capture/replay techniques have been developed to address the limitation of the traditional methods.

2.2 Capture/Replay Using Image Recognition

Sikuli [12] is a tool that incorporates image recognition in capture/replay to provide a robust GUI testing tool. Testing using Sikuli consists of a capture phase and replay phase, similar to traditional capture/replay techniques.

During the capture phase the tester executes a GUI testcase. The capture tool of Sikuli records the *visible content* of the screen around the location where the GUI event is expected. It records a sequence of screen content at the locations where the tester executes the events. During the replay phase, the replay tool uses the recorded screen contents to identify the location of the application where the events needs to be executed.

Using the screen content to identify the location of an event, instead of the screen coordinates, has the distinct advantage of being tolerant of changes in location of GUI widgets. The replay tool is able to handle changes in the location of the application's windows as well as changes in the location of its widgets.

A testcase, *T*, identical to that in Fig. 2A is recorded by Sikuli. Fig. 3A shows the information recorded by Sikuli during the capture phase. In this figure an image of the screen content around the location of the event is recorded. This corresponds to the image of the widgets square, create, exit, and yes.

Fig. 3B shows how the replay tool of Sikuli replays a GUI event on the application. In this figure the replay tool searches for the image recorded during the square event. Image recognition techniques are used to search for the recorded image in the visible GUI of the application. The replay tool locates the images on the windows of the Radio Button Demo application and executes the event. Had the windows of the application moved during the replay phase, the replay tool would have successfully located the create widget. In addition the testcase can be replayed successfully in a different visual environment, for example, by using a screen with different resolution.

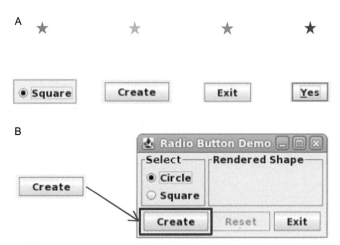

Fig. 3 Capture/replay method for creating a GUI testcase for the Radio Button Demo application. (A) The *capture* tool creates the testcase as a set of screen contents where GUI events are executed. (B) The *replay* tool identifies the target location for an event using the captured screen contents.

2.3 Finite State Machine

Esmelioglu *et al.* [13] have modeled the GUI of a GUI-based application as a *finite state machine* (FSM). An FSM is defined as $FSM = (S, I, O, T, \Phi)$, where S is the set of finite GUI states, I is the set of inputs to the GUI, O is the finite set of outputs, T is the transition function $S \times I \rightarrow S$ defining the next state based on the current state and input, and Φ is the output function $S \times I \rightarrow O$ defining the output from a transition.

An FSM for the `Radio Button Demo` application is shown in Fig. 4. In this example, each state represents four GUI elements—L, E, C, S, where $L = 0/1$ indicates that w_6 is (un)checked, $E = 0/1$ indicates that the `Exit Confirmation` window is closed/opened, $C = 0/1$ indicates that a shape is cleared/rendered, $S = C/S$ indicates that a circle/square radio button has been selected.

A testcase can be created from the FSM model by traversing it from the *root*. A depth-first or breadth-first walk may be employed. When the traversal routine encounters a state, all input events from that state to the root state are emitted as event sequences of a testcase. The maximum depth to be traversed is an input to the traversal routine. It determines the maximum length of the testcase. In Fig. 4 the root node is labeled as `start`. A depth-first

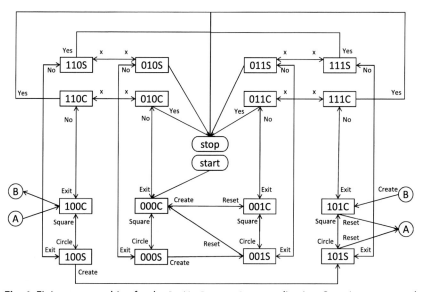

Fig. 4 Finite state machine for the `Radio Button Demo` application. State is represented with *LECS*—*L* create log, *E* `Exit Confirmation` window opened, *C* shape created, *S* circle/square selected. Transitions are labeled as: *SRC* → *DST*, with *input* marked at tail.

traversal along the path 000C → 000S → 001S → 000C would create square → create → reset as a length-3 testcase. The traversal routine may choose to skip exploring states that are already encountered along the traversal path.

Deploying an FSM for modeling a GUI and creating testcases suffers from certain practical problems. First, the FSM may require a large number of states to represent the GUI. This is tedious to create, both manually and automatically, and also difficult to maintain for a GUI under development or maintenance. The states and transitions may be difficult to map onto the actual GUI, resulting in greater maintenance effort. The total number of testcases of a given length grows rapidly with increasing value of the length. This results in a large number of testcases in the testsuite that needs to be prioritized by the tester.

2.4 Variable Finite State Machine

Variable finite state machine (VFSM) is a technique employed by Shehady *et al.* [4] to represent the GUI states of a GUI-based application. The authors show that VFSMs require fewer states to represent the GUI, are more intuitive for representing a GUI, and can be used to create testcases and detect faults in a GUI-based application.

The key difference between FSM and VFSM is that VFSMs use of a set of global *variables*. The current value of these variables affect state transitions that in turn may alter the value of the variables.

A VFSM is represented as a 7-tuple, $VFSM = (S, I, O, T, \Phi, V, \zeta)$. The symbols S, I, O posses the same semantics and properties as described for FSM (see Section 2.3). In addition, V is a set of n variables defined as $V = \{V_1, V_2, ..., V_n\}$, where each V_i is a set of values the i-th global variable may assume. T is a state transition function, $T = D_T \rightarrow S$; Φ is an output function, $\Phi = D_T \rightarrow O$; where $D_T \in S \times I \times V_1 \times V_2 \times \cdots \times V_n$. This indicates that the state transitions, T and the output function Φ both are function of the global variables V. In addition, ζ is a state transition function that determines if the state of the global variables are altered as the result of a transition.

Fig. 5 shows the VFSM for the Radio Button Demo application. In this figure, the state component C has been removed and is modeled with the variable V. A transition is labeled as *precondition→effect*, where the transition takes place only if the precondition is true with the postcondition being affected after the transition. A transition from the state 00C to 01C takes place on the input event exit. A transition from 00C to itself may be effected by the input event create resulting in the variable V being set to 1. It may also be effected by the input event reset if the variable V contained 1. After the transition V is set to 0.

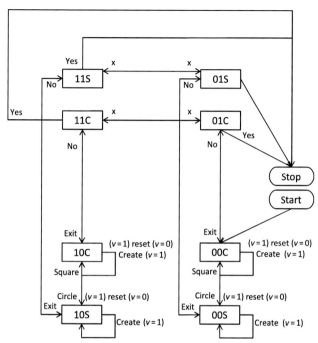

Fig. 5 Variable finite state machine for the `Radio Button Demo` application. State is represented with *LES—L* create log, *E* `Exit Confirmation` window opened, *S* circle/square selected. Transitions are labeled as: (*precondition*)*SRC* → *DST*(*effect*), with *input* marked at tail. The variable *V* models the *created* state.

VFSMs produce smaller state machine that are more compact than FSMs, while retaining a similar state space. The VFSM is converted into an equivalent FSM in order to create testcases. This is done by expanding the set of states, *S* and set of transitions, *T* using *V* and Φ.

2.5 Complete Interaction Sequence

White *et al.* [5] use complete interaction sequence (CIS) as a method to reduce the state space of a GUI-based application. The authors define a GUI *responsibility* as a GUI activity consisting of GUI objects that produces an observable effect on the GUI's environment—memory usage, peripheral device activity, underlying business logic response. A responsibility is identified manually by the tester. For each identified responsibility, the sequence of GUI events that lead to that responsibility is called the complete interaction sequence for that responsibility.

Using this method the FSM of a CIS from the GUI-based application is reduced to a *reducedFSM*. This is done by (1) manually identifying the GUI responsibilities in a GUI-based application, (2) identifying the CIS for each responsibility, (3) creating an FSM for a CIS, (4) converting an FSM to a *reduced* FSM, and (5) testing a CIS using the reduced FSM to generate and execute testcases on the GUI-based application.

The FSM is converted into the reduced FSM by identifying *subFSM*s in the FSM for the CIS. A set of states $S = \{S_1, ..., S_n\}$ in an FSM form a subFSM if there exists a directed path from S_i to S_j, for every $S_i, S_j \in S$. In addition, a subFSM S possesses *structural symmetry* if (1) in S, there exists states S_1 with only one incoming transition and S_2 with only one outgoing transition and there exists multiple paths from S_1 to S_2, (2) states outside S do not affect transitions within S, and (3) choice of paths taken between S_1 and S_2 do not affect states outside S.

A subFSM with structural symmetry can be replaced with a single *superstate* in the FSM. The subFSM can now be tested in isolation. Identification and replacement of subFSMs reduce the overall complexity of the FSM for a CIS, resulting in a *reduced FSM*. The reduced FSM can also be tested by using any one path through a subFSM when its superstate is encountered in the reduced FSM.

2.6 Off-Nominal Finite State Machine

While most model-based GUI testing methods attempt to generate and execute testcases that invoke valid event sequences in the GUI of a GUI-based application, testing the GUI for invalid event sequences is also important. These testcases form a *negative* testsuite that verifies that the GUI does not permit a user to execute disallowed actions. Intuitively, generating invalid event sequences from a graph model of a GUI is straightforward. One needs to select an event-pair that does not share an edge and generate a testcase which contains this pair as an event sequence.

Belli *et al.* [6] generate testcases for event sequences that are invalid. They argue that these sequences should be tested in addition to valid sequences. A CIS (see Section 2.5) is used for creating a *faulty complete interaction sequence* (FCIS). Given a GUI, a CIS and its corresponding FSM with valid transitions is constructed. Missing edges in the FSM, termed *Faulty Interaction Pairs* (FIPs), are identified. A testcase containing an FIP can be easily generated by first generating a testcase leading to the first event in the FIP. This testcase is then prefixed to the FIP, creating a testcase with an invalid event sequence.

2.7 Event-Flow Graph

The Event-Flow Graph [9] is a GUI model, of a GUI-based application, that represents GUI events, and their sequences, that can be executed on the GUI. The Event-Flow Graph is a directed graph, where a vertex represents an *event* executable on the GUI. An edge $e_i \rightarrow e_j$ from vertex i to j indicates that the event j is executable *immediately* after executing event i. Event j is said to *follow* event i. Intuitively, the Event-Flow Graph models the possible execution paths on the GUI.

Formally, an Event-Flow Graph is defined as a triple $\langle V, E, B \rangle$, where V is a set of vertices representing events on the GUI of a GUI-based application; $E \in V \times V$ is a set of directed edges representing the follows relation; $B \in V$ is a set of vertices representing *initial events*, events that are available for execution immediately after the application is launched.

The Event-Flow Graph for the Radio Button Demo application is shown in Fig. 6. In this figure, events are shown as ovals, shaded ovals represent initial events and directed edges represent the follows relation. *Terminal*

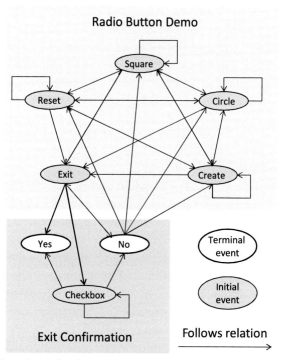

Fig. 6 Event-Flow Graph for the Radio Button Demo application.

events are events that close a model GUI window of the application. They are shown in white ovals.

From Fig. 6 it can be seen that event *yes* can be executed after *exit*, that is, *yes* follows *exit*. However, *yes* cannot be executed after *create*. The events *yes* and *no* are terminal events since they close the application and the Exit Confirmation modal window, respectively. Valid testcases can be easily generated by traversing the Event-Flow Graph starting from an initial state, for example, *square → create → circle → exit → yes*.

The Event-Flow Graph of a GUI-based application can be extracted from the run-time state of the GUI, by a process of reverse engineering [14]. In this process, a monitor application, called the *GUI Ripper* launches the application, identifies its top-level windows and initial GUI states, executes all visible events, and continues identifying new windows that may be created. The GUI Ripper continues the process of executing events and extracting the GUI state of windows until as much of the GUI as possible has been traversed. This Event-Flow Graph is an approximation to the complete Event-Flow Graph, since the GUI Ripper may miss out some GUI windows and widgets [14].

The Event-Flow Graph represents valid executable event sequences on the GUI. Testcases can be easily generated from the Event-Flow Graph using different graph traversal algorithms starting from the initial events. Examples of graph traversal algorithms are goal-directed [15], random-walk [7]. Graph-pruning techniques based on the GUI's behavior such as EIG [7] and ESIG [8] may also be used to reduce the state space of the Event-Flow Graph.

2.8 Event-Interaction Graph

The Event-Flow Graph models all events and all possible event-sequences on the GUI. For typical GUI's the number of event sequences of a given length can grow exponentially even with small event sequence lengths. This leads to large testsuites with impractical execution times.

Xie *et al.* [9] empirically developed a method to prune the state space of the EFG. This increased the feasibility of generating testsuites with longer testcases and practical suite sizes. In their study the authors empirically concluded that *structural GUI events*—open/close menu item, open/close modeless windows—typically do not reveal defects in the application. This is likely because these events are typically executed by popular libraries that are well tested and defect-free. On the other hand, *termination events*—where modal windows are closed—and *system interaction events*—where the GUI interacts with the underlying business logic—are more likely to reveal defects. The Event-Interaction Graph models this logic.

Intuitively, an Event-Interaction Graph contains only *termination* and *system interaction* events. An edge, $x \to y$, between two events, x and y, indicate that event y is executable (not necessarily immediately) after event x. The edges in the Event-Interaction Graph models the *interacts with* relation.

An Event-Interaction Graph can be easily derived from an Event-Flow Graph based on GUI properties of each event [16]. The Event-Interaction Graph for the Radio Button Demo application is shown in Fig. 7. This was obtained from the Event-Flow Graph by removing the *exit* event, since this event opens a modal window and is classified as a structural event. Inbounds edges to the *exit* event are connected to all the events of its outbound edges.

Testcases are generated from the Event-Interaction Graph using graph traversal algorithms. Testcases generated directly from the Event-Interaction Graph may need to be augmented with missing structural events (such as the exit event) in order to make the testcase executable on the GUI.

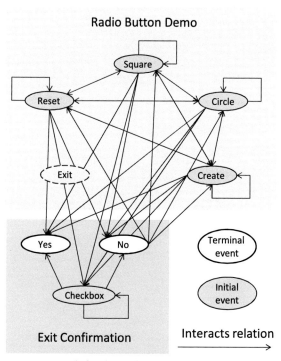

Fig. 7 Event-Interaction Graph for the Radio Button Demo application.

2.9 Event-Semantic Interaction Graph

The GUI model represented using an Event-Interaction Graph can be further pruned based on semantic relationship between GUI widgets. Yuan *et al.* [8] created a sparse graph, where an edge was present between two GUI events only if executing the first event influenced the execution result of the second event. The resulting representation called Event-Semantic Interaction Graph (ESIG) greatly reduced the state space and was useful for generating longer testcases with a practical testsuite size (Fig. 8).

Intuitively, if executing an event *x* affects the visible result of executing event *y*, then they are likely to share common program code or program state. In the Radio Button Demo application, the event handlers for the events *square* and *create* share common program state in the variables created and currentShape. As a result, executing the event sequences—(1) *square* in isolation, (2) *create* in isolation, and (3) *square → create*—show different resulting visible states on the GUI (Fig. 9). In this figure, (A) is the initial state of the application. The resulting visible states after executing the events

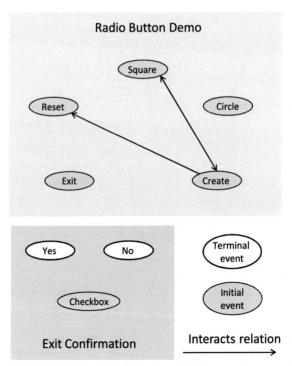

Fig. 8 Event-Semantic Interaction Graph for the Radio Button Demo application.

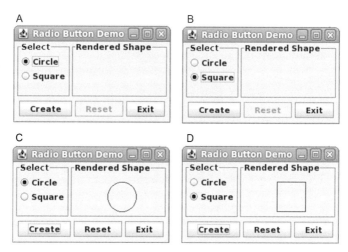

Fig. 9 ESI relationship. (A) Initial application state; (B) *square* executed; (C) *create* executed; (D) *square → create* executed in sequence. Comparing (C) and (D) the event *square* influences the behavior of the event *create*.

square, *create*, and *square→create* are shown in (B), (C), and (D), respectively. The event *square*, when executed before the event *create*, makes the latter behave differently. This can be deduced by comparing the GUI states in Fig. 9C and D. As a result the event *square* is said to interact with the event *create*.

Such interacting events, in a GUI, can be identified and modeled as an *Event-Semantic Interaction Graph* (ESIG). The ESIG for the Radio Button Demo application is shown in Fig. 8. As expected, there is an edge from the event *square* to the event *create*. Comparing Figs. 6, 7, and 8 it can be seen that the ESIG is sparse compared to the EFG or EIG. The ESIG has fewer edges compared to the EFG and EIG. It is because not all event-pairs from the EFG or EIG interact with each other.

Testcases may be generated from the ESIG by traversing the graph using a depth-first or breadth-first walk. Since the ESIG is sparse it is possible to generate testcases of a longer length within a testsuite of reasonable size. The ESIG-based testcases specifically target parts of the application that interact with each other. These testcases specifically target complex defects that require interacting events to be exercised together.

2.10 Planning

Plan generation [15] has been used by Memon *et al.* to generate testcases for GUI-based applications. This is a goal-driven approach where the tester creates testcases by specifying the intended GUI task to be performed. The test generator produces the sequence of events that brings the application from the given *initial state* to the required *goal state*.

The intuition in developing goal-driven testcase generation is that testers often find it easier to specify *what* needs to be done rather than *how* it needs to be done. Often, a GUI might present more than one, often convoluted, path for performing a task, that a tester may fail to test. Plan generation takes as input the starting GUI state and produces all possible paths for reaching the desired goal GUI state.

Generating testcases using plan generation works in two phases. In the first phase, the tester uses domain knowledge of the GUI to create *precondition* and *effect* plan operators. Plan operators are building blocks for defining state transitions in the GUI. An operator models the state of GUI entities that may trigger the operator. It also defines the effect of the operator on the state of GUI entities. In the second phase, the tester identifies tasks that need to be performed on the GUI by specifying the initial and goal state of the GUI. Thereafter, a plan generator, such as an AI planner, uses the plan operators and tasks to produce a set of testcases for each task.

Fig. 10A shows an initial and goal state of the `Radio Button Demo` application. There are many paths, in theory infinite, of transitioning the GUI from this initial state to goal state. The tester can specify a testing goal with this pair of states. The planner will generate a testcase shown in Fig. 10B. Fig. 10C shows an example a plan operators for this GUI.

2.11 Genetic Algorithm

Testcases on a GUI are sequences of events. It is possible to model a testcase as a *gene*, where each event is an *allele* (or chromosome). The goal of the genetic algorithm is to produce a set of event sequences that satisfy a *good* testing or coverage criteria.

Kasik *et al.* [17] have applied genetic algorithms to generate GUI testcases. In this work, the authors have attempted to emulate the event sequence a novice user would execute on the GUI. They argue that a novice user would typically execute more events on the GUI in order to achieve a task than an expert user. The novice user's event sequence would execute unpredictable paths that the developer would not have predicted. This could thus trigger untested execution sequences and hence reveal defects in the GUI.

The algorithm begins creating a set of initial alleles, generating a *reward* score for each allele, replicating *good* alleles to the next generation of genes, applying mutation and crossover operators to enable better exploration of the search space. The goal of the genetic algorithm is to promote testcases

A

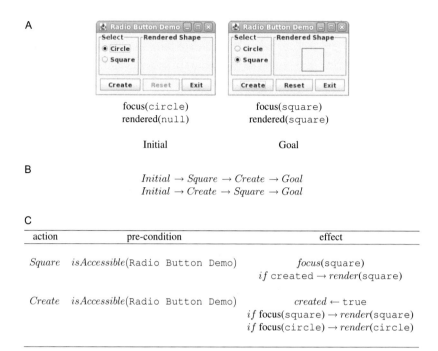

focus(circle)   focus(square)
rendered(null)   rendered(square)

Initial   Goal

B

$Initial \rightarrow Square \rightarrow Create \rightarrow Goal$
$Initial \rightarrow Create \rightarrow Square \rightarrow Goal$

C

action	pre-condition	effect
Square	*isAccessible*(Radio Button Demo)	*focus*(square) *if* created → *render*(square)
Create	*isAccessible*(Radio Button Demo)	*created* ← true *if* focus(square) → *render*(square) *if* focus(circle) → *render*(circle)

Fig. 10 Plan generation for Radio Button Demo application. (A) Initial and goal states for creating a testcase. (B) Two plans created for testing the goal. (C) Plan operators for creating testcases for the GUI.

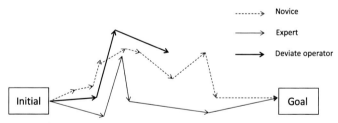

Fig. 11 Genetic algorithm emulating a novice user's behavior to generate GUI testcase.

that best resemble novice users. In this work, the authors claim that devising the best reward strategy for the alleles was a challenge. The reward system implemented a *deviate* strategy from the expert user's path to emulate novice users.

Fig. 11 shows a typical path traversed by an expert user and by a novice user, to complete the same task. The genetic algorithm attempts to emulate the novice user by rewarding events that make the testcase *deviate* from the expert user's path.

2.12 Covering Arrays

Yuan *et al.* [18] use *covering arrays* to generate long testcases. This approach can be used for testing an event in the *context* of other events. This is because an event, e_1, may behave differently when executed after another event e_2. In addition, a set of events, e_1, e_2 may behave differently when another event e_3 is executed before either of them.

A *covering array*, $CA(N; t, k, v)$, is an $N \times k$ array on a set of v symbols such that every $N \times t$ subarray contains all ordered subsets of all v symbols, at least once. This means that any t-columns of the array will contain all t-combinations of the v symbols. Using covering arrays, testcases are generated for testing the execution of a set of v events in t-way interaction such that each event occurs at each position in length-k testcases.

The testcase generation workflow operates by partitioning a GUI of a GUI-based application. Typically, a GUI window forms a partition. Each event in a partition is considered as a symbol in v. Thereafter, testcases of length k are generated by creating a covering array of dimension $N \times k$. Each row of this array is a testcase. N, the number generated testcases, is minimized using optimization techniques. The final output is a set of N, length-k testcases.

Table 3 shows all 2-way interaction of events in the `Radio Button Demo` application's `Exit Conformation` window (partition) with three events— *yes*, *no*, and *(un)check*. Length-4 testcase are generated to test the effect of placing each event at sequence location 1 through 4. To test the placement of 3 events in all positions of a length-4 testcase, $P_3^4 = 81$ testcases are required. However, using a covering array, $CA(9; 2, 4, 3)$, only 9 testcases are required.

2.13 Summary

Capture/replay is a popular method for testing the GUI of a GUI-based application. It enables testers with domain knowledge of the application to create visually guided testcases.

Model-based testing of the GUI of GUI-based applications have received considerable attention over the past decade [19]. Most techniques create a representation of the GUI based on automated or manual analysis of the GUI. Subsequently, testcases for testing the GUI are generated based on this representation. Researchers have focused on (1) obtaining a concise and accurate representation of the GUI, (2) developing state space reduction techniques, and (3) studying the generation of effective testcases based on the model.

Table 3 Covering Array *CA*(9; 2, 4, 3) for the `Exit Confirmation` Window of `Radio Button Demo` Application

yes	*yes*	*yes*	*yes*	*yes*	*yes*
yes	*no*	*yes*	*no*	*no*	*(un)check*
yes	*(un)check*	*yes*	*(un)check*	*(un)check*	*no*
no	*no*	*no*	*no*	*yes*	*no*
no	*(un)check*	*no*	*(un)check*	*no*	*yes*
no	*yes*	*no*	*yes*	*(un)check*	*(un)check*
(un)check	*(un)check*	*(un)check*	*(un)check*	*yes*	*(un)check*
(un)check	*yes*	*(un)check*	*yes*	*no*	*no*
(un)check	*no*	*(un)check*	*no*	*(un)check*	*yes*
2-way interaction		*CA*(9; 2, 4, 3) testcases			

Only 9 testcases are required for testing 2-way interaction of 3 events at all 4 positions in a testcase. Exhaustive testing would require 81 Testcases.

The next section describes a model-based method for generating long GUI testcases. This method leverages interactions between the program code of GUI event handlers.

3. INTERACTING GUI EVENTS

GUI defects are often revealed when a GUI event is exercised in combination with other GUI events. These defects are often complex in nature and are revealed by the execution of targeted event sequences. Identifying sequences of GUI events that reveal such defects is a challenging task.

Event–Code Interaction is a paradigm that identifies events in a GUI-based application that *interact* at the program code level. The interacting events may be combined to created an Event–Code Interaction Graph (ECIG). Testcases created from the ECIG target specific parts of the GUI specially those that interact with each other.

This section describes Event–Code Interaction which is a method for identifying interacting GUI events and combining them to create testcases.

3.1 Event–Code Interaction

An event in a GUI-based application is typically associated with an *event handler*. An event handler is a program function that is executed by the application or operating system when an event is executed on the application. This function may in turn execute other functions, spawn threads, and trigger timer-based code execution. Hence, an application-level event causes a set of lines of program code to be executed in the application and possibly in the platform. Different events will trigger their own event handlers to be executed. The program code executed in response to different events may contain shared pieces of code. They may also share application state such as objects and data structures that are accessed by the event handler when an event is executed.

Shared program code and program state between different event handlers create a possibility of *interactions* between them. For example:

Program code: An event handler may acquire a lock that is also required by another event handler sharing code. Hence, execution of one event handler may delay the execution of the other event handler.

Program state: An event handler may modify an object required by another event handler. This modification may affect the execution of the other event handler.

An event e_1, belonging to an application under test, A, is said to interact with another event e_2, belonging to A, at a program code level, if the execution of event e_1 alters the lines of code executed by event e_2. This interaction is represented as an edge $e_1 \rightarrow e_2$ from event e_1 to event e_2.

An ECIG is a graph representing ECI relations between the events of an application under test, A. In this graph, vertices represent events belonging to the GUI of the application. An edge is present from an event e_1 to another event e_2 if there exists an ECI relation from e_1 to e_2.

Definition. An Event–Code Interaction Graph, *ECIG*, for an application under test is defined as a triple, $ECIG = (V, E, I)$, where:

1. $V = \{v_1, \ldots, v_n\}$ is a set of n vertices such that each vertex represents an event in the application under test.
2. $E = \{e_1, \ldots, e_m\}$ and $E \in V \times V$ is a set of m directed edges. A directed edge e from vertex v_1 to v_2, represented by $v_1 \rightarrow v_2$, represents an ECI relation between events represented by the vertices v_1 and v_2.
3. $I \subseteq V$ is a set of vertices representing *initial* events that are executable immediately after the application is launched.   □

Fig. 12 shows the ECIG for the `Radio Button Demo` application. In this figure, $V = \{square, circle, create, exit, reset, yes, no, checkbox\}$, $E = \{square \rightarrow create, circle \rightarrow create, create \rightarrow square, create \rightarrow circle\}$, $I = \{square, circle, create, exit, reset\}$.

Algorithm. Given an application on which events can be executed, a simple algorithm can be followed to determine if one of its event, e_1, interacts with another of its event, e_2:

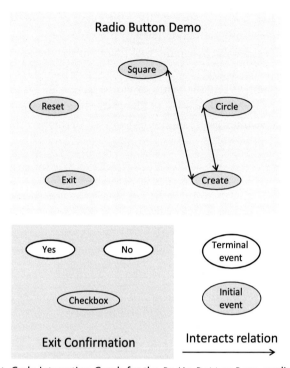

Fig. 12 Event–Code Interaction Graph for the `Radio Button Demo` application.

$e_1 \to e_2$: Execute event e_1 as the first event immediately after launching the application. This might require *initial events* to be executed in order to reach the event e_1. Follow e_1 immediately with event e_2. Record the lines of code executed by event handler for e_2—call it set X.

e_2: Execute event e_2 as the first event immediately after launching the application. This might require *initial events* to be executed in order to reach the event e_2. Record the lines of code executed by the event handler of e_2—call it set Y.

ECI predicates: The following three predicates indicate whether the execution of event e_1 interacts with the execution of event e_2.

1. $X - Y \neq \Phi$. This indicates that certain lines of code were executed when the sequence $e_1 \to e_2$ was executed (X) but were not executed when e_2 was executed in isolation (Y).

2. $Y - X \neq \Phi$. This indicates that certain lines of code were executed when e_2 was executed in isolation (Y) but were not executed when the sequence $e_1 \to e_2$ was executed (X).

3. $X \neq Y$. This condition indicates that the lines of code executed by e_2 in isolation and by $e_1 \to e_2$ are identical. However, there exists a set of lines, for which the hit count between X and Y is different.

If ECI predicates 1, 2, or 3 are true then the event e_1 is said to interact with the event e_2 at the program code level.   □

Example. Consider the program code fragment for the Radio Button Demo application in Table 4. The code in the upper box is part of the event handler for the *circle* event. It sets the value of currentShape to Shape.CIRCLE. The initial value of currentShape is null. The lower box shows part of the event handler for the event *create*. Columns (A) and (B) of this box show the line of code executed in two different conditions:

A: Shows the lines of code executed by the event handler for *create* when the event sequence *circle→create* is executed after launching the application.

B: Shows the lines of code executed by the event handler for *create* when the event *create* is executed after launching the application.

Table 4 Top: Event Handler for the Event Circle; Bottom: Part of the Event Handler for the Create Event of the Radio Button Demo Application

Event handler for the event Circle

```
class W1Listener implements ActionListener {
    @Override
    public void actionPerformed(ActionEvent arg0) {
        currentShape = Shape.CIRCLE;
        if (created)
            draw(new CirclePanel());
```

A B	Radio Button Demo
— —	class W3Listener implements ActionListener {
— —	@Override
— —	public void actionPerformed(ActionEvent e) {
— —	JPanel shape;
X X	if (currentShape == Shape.CIRCLE ||
— —	currentShape == Shape.SQUARE)
X —	w5.setEnabled(true);
— —	
X X	created = true;
X X	if (currentShape == Shape.CIRCLE)
X —	shape = new CirclePanel();
— X	else if (currentShape == Shape.SQUARE)
— —	shape = new SquarePanel();
— —	else
— X	shape = new EmptyPanel();
X X	drawShape();

It can be seen that the lines of code executed by the event *create* in isolation (B) are different from the lines of code executed by the same event handler when the event sequence *circle→create* (A). The state variable currentShape affects the execution of *create* in (A). The program state currentShape is set to Shape.CIRCLE by the event *circle* influencing the event *create* to execute different lines of code. This example shows that the event *circle* interacts with the event *create*. Hence an edge *circle→create* will be added to the ECIG for the Radio Button Demo application in Fig. 12. The other three remaining edges are added based on a similar observation.   □

Some event pairs do not have any ECI relations. For example, the event *square* does not interact with the event *circle*. The lines of code executed by the event handler for *circle* when the event sequence *square→circle* is executed is identical to that when *circle* is executed in isolation. Hence the event *square* has no interaction with the event *circle*.

3.2 Composite Event–Code Interaction

The concept of Event–Code Interaction, where an event e_1 interacts with another event e_2, can be extended to *composite events*.

Definition. A composite event, CE, in an application under test, is defined as an ordered set of events, $\{E_1, E_2, ..., E_n\}$ where each constituent event E_i, for $1 \leq i \leq n$, is executed in sequence without executing any other event in between two successive constituent event.   □

Composite ECI predicates. A composite event $CE_1 = \{E_1, E_2, ..., E_n\}$ is said to interact with another event e_2 of the application under test, at the program code level, if both the following predicates are true:

- The execution of the composite event CE_1 alters the lines of code executed by the event e_2.
- There are no ECI relations for any ordered subset of CE_1 ($E_1→e_2$, ..., $E_n→e_2$, $\{E_1, E_2\} → e_2$, and so on).

Intuitively, this means that a set of constituent events independently do not interact with another event e_2. However, when the constituent events are executed as a composite event, their combined execution does interact with the event e_2.   □

Example. Consider the Radio Button Demo application example. Composite events in this application of different lengths are like—$\{circle, create\}$ of length-2, $\{create, exit, no\}$ of length-3, $\{create, circle, reset, exit\}$ of length-4.

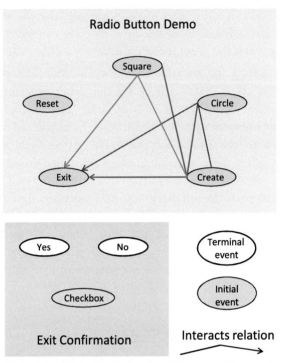

Fig. 13 Event–Code Interaction Graph for length-2 composite events in the `Radio Button Demo` **application.**

For simplicity of description, consider composite events of length-2. Fig. 13 shows the *interacts* relation of the `Radio Button Demo` application with length-2 composite events. The following three sets of *interacts* relations were empirically determined

1. {*create, circle*} →*exit*

2. {*create, square*} →*exit*

3. {*square, create*} →*exit*; {*circle, create*} →*exit*

In this figure, each set from the list above is shown in a distinct color. An *interacts* relation is shown as a set of two edges with the same color. The first edge is undirected and connects the two vertices of the composite event. The second edge is directed and connect the last event of the composite event and the interacting event. For example, the composite event {*circle, create*} interacts with *exit*. It is shown as *circle—create→exit*. In this example, none of the constituent events—*create, circle, square*—of the composite events interact with the event *exit*. □

This section describes Event–Code Interaction and the Event–Code Interaction Graph. Event–Code Interaction is a paradigm for identifying GUI events that interact at the program code level. The next section compares three GUI models, namely EFG, EIG, and ECIG, by modeling the GUI of four subject applications.

4. COMPARING GUI MODELS

Characteristics of the Event-Flow Graph, Event-Interaction Graph, and Event–Code Interaction Graph are demonstrated using four open-source GUI-based applications. It is shown that EFG and EIG-based testcases are suitable for rapid-testing or smoke testing a GUI-based application while ECIG-based testcases are suitable for testing deeper interactions between GUI events. Applications that are used for demonstration are the following:

1. **ArgoUML:** An open-source[a] software design and engineering tool.
2. **Buddi:** An open-source[b] personal finance and budgeting software.
3. **JabRef:** An open-source[c] software for managing bibliography references.
4. **JEdit:** An open-source[d] text editor for computer programmers.

Properties of the applications are shown in Table 5. In this table, the column *Version* shows the version number of the application that was selected for evaluation. The column *Year* shows the year when the application was first made available. All the applications have been present for a decade or more, indicating that an appreciable amount of code maturity would have been reached. The column *LOC* shows the number of lines of code in the application. The applications are nontrivial in terms of code size.

Table 5 Properties of Applications that are Used for Demonstration

Application	Abbreviation	Version	Year	LOC
ArgoUML	AU	0.34	1999	70,430
Buddi	BD	3.4.1.11	2006	155,960
JabRef	JA	2.10	2003	61,714
JEdit	JE	5.1.0	1998	67,761

[a] http://www.tigris.org.
[b] http://buddi.digitalcave.ca.
[c] http://jabref.sourceforge.net.
[d] http://www.jedit.org.

Three GUI models are constructed for each application. The models are EFG, EIG, and ECIG (see Sections 2.7, 2.8, and 3 for a description of these models).

The EFG model is constructed by the process of reverse engineering described in Section 2.7. This process extracts structural information of the GUI from the run-time state of the application. It identifies executable *events* and *follows* relationship between events. The *events* and *follows* relations are modeled as an EFG. Vertices in the EFG represent executable GUI events. Edges in the EFG represent *follows* relation between events. Table 6 lists the number of vertices (column *V ertices*) and edges (column *Edges*) in the EFG for each application.

The EIG model is constructed from the EFG by retaining terminal and system interaction events (vertices). An edge is added from one event to another if the succeeding event can be executed by traversing *any* path from the preceding event (see Section 2.8). Table 6 lists the number of vertices (column *V ertices*) and edges (column *Edges*) in the EIG for each application.

The ECIG model is constructed from the EIG using the method described in Section 3. The number of vertices and edges in the ECIG is shown in Table 6.

The graph models constructed for the applications are shown in Figs. 14 and 15. In these two figures the EFG, EIG, and ECIG for an application are shown in a row. From Table 6 and Figs. 14 and 15 it can be seen that the ECIG contains fewer vertices and edges than the EFG and EIG. In other words, the ECIG is a sparse graph compared to the EFG and EIG. A sparse graph has certain advantages compared to a dense graph.

GUI testcases may be created from a graph model by traversing the graph in a depth or breadth-first manner. When a desired depth has been reached, the path from the root to the vertex being traversed is emitted as a GUI testcase. If the graph is dense then the number of paths (or testcases in a

Table 6 Count of Vertices and Edges for EFG, EIG, and ECIG Models

Application	EFG		EIG		ECIG	
	# Vertices	# Edges	# Vertices	# Edges	# Vertices	# Edges
AU	498	15,846	313	67,445	205	799
BD	245	3,621	144	12,576	45	157
JA	367	12,981	276	57,873	168	355
JE	428	13,687	378	133,734	224	517

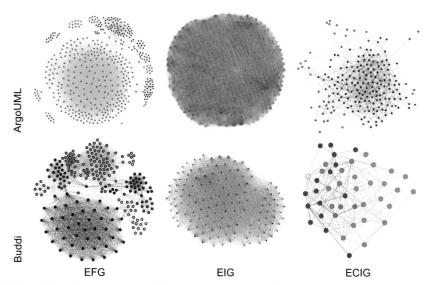

Fig. 14 Visual representation of the EFG, EIG, and ECIG of ArgoUML and Buddi. The EFG represents *follows* relation between all pairs of events. EIG represents *follows* relation between nonstructural events. It contains fewer vertices and more edges. ECIG is a subset of the EIG, containing edges that interact at the program code level.

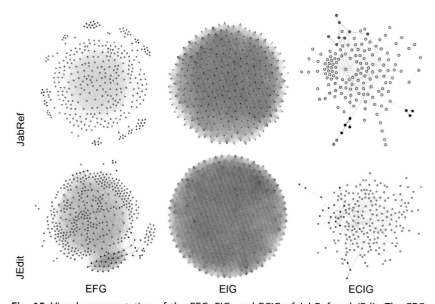

Fig. 15 Visual representation of the EFG, EIG, and ECIG of JabRef and JEdit. The EFG represents *follows* relation between all pairs of events. EIG represents *follows* relation between nonstructural events. It contains fewer vertices and more edges. ECIG is a subset of the EIG, containing edges that interact at the program code level.

testsuite) of a given length may be very large. Sometimes, it is too large to execute within a practical time. On the other hand, if the graph is sparse then the number of paths (or testcases) of a given length may be reasonable. Such a reasonably sized testsuite may be executable in a practical timeframe.

Table 7 lists the testsuite size, for ArgoUML, in a testsuite for testcase lengths from 2 to 7. The testsuite size is shown for the three models— EFG, EIG, and ECIG. Since the EFG and EIG are dense graphs, the testsuite size rapidly increases. In fact beyond a length of 3 the testsuite size is too large to execute within a practical time. Since the ECIG is a sparse graph, the testsuite size is reasonably small for testcase lengths up to 7. Going beyond length 7, Table 8 shows the testsuite size for testsuites created from the ECIG model for ArgoUML. Testcases with lengths up to 14 are created with reasonably sized testsuites.

The dense nature of EFG and EIG lends them to creating a large number of testcases. When restricted to testcases with a short length of 2 or 3, a reasonably sized testsuite is obtained. These short-length testcases serve as *smoke tests* for the application. Smoke tests are used to rapidly test the application for defects and regression.

A testcase with a length of more than 3 events is considered to be a long testcase. Long GUI testcase are better than short length-2 testcases since they are good at exercising deeper interactions between GUI events and hence are good at revealing complex defects. The sparse nature of ECIG makes it easy to create long testcases. The size of an ECIG-based testsuite with long testcases remains small making it easy to execute within a reasonable time.

The ECIG is created based on program code level interactions between GUI events. Testcases created from the ECIG therefore exercise specific parts of the application that interact with each other at the program code

Table 7 Testsuite Size for Testcase Created From the EFG, EIG, and ECIG Models

Length	EFG	EIG	ECIG
2	15,846	67,445	—
3	678,628	13,520,515	319
4	30,421,680	2,696,435,575	797
5	1,377,291,937	537,280,797,376	1074
6	62,464,993,710	—	1801
7	2,833,714,733,116	—	2225

Length of testcases in a testsuite is chosen as 2, 3, 4, 5, 6, 7.

Table 8 Testsuite Size for Testcases Created
From the ECIG Model for ArgoUML

Length	ECIG
8	2247
9	2546
10	2522
11	2789
12	2660
13	2585
14	2089

Length of testcases in a testsuite is chosen between
8 and 14.

level. Exercising these deep interactions often requires specially crafted long testcase. ECIG-based long testcases are a method to exercise these deep interactions.

This section compares three GUI models namely, EFG, EIG, and ECIG. Characteristics of the models and testcases created from these models are compared. The EFG and EIG models are suitable for creating short GUI testcases that serve as smoke tests. The ECIG is good for creating long GUI testcases that are good at revealing deeper GUI defects.

5. CONCLUSION

A defect-free GUI makes a GUI-based application reliable, robust, secure, and user-friendly. Verifying the GUI is an important part of the development cycle of a GUI-based software. At present capture and replay-based GUI verification techniques are popular. Over the last decade there has been a growing interest in automated model-based verification methods. Models such as finite state machines and Event-Flow Graph-based models have been used to exercise deep interactions in the GUI of GUI-based software.

A wide spectrum of devices employs GUIs as an interface to interact with the user. GUI-based devices range from low-cost readers to high-performance supercomputers. Increasingly GUI-based devices operate in an interconnected manner, for example, mobile computing devices, phones, wearable devices, home monitoring systems, automated manufacturing systems, and motor vehicles. This necessitates rigorous verification of the GUI as well as the interaction of a GUI with the software on connected devices. With connected devices the state space of the software and its GUI grows owing to the vast scope of interaction between the devices. Verifying the operation of a GUI of interconnected devices in a large state space using manual methods is prone to human errors.

Model-based verification methods that efficiently and effectively prune the state space of the GUI is necessary for verifying the GUI software on interconnected devices. Models such as EFG, EIG, ESIG, and ECIG effectively model the GUI enabling the tester to create smoke tests as well as testcases that exercise deep GUI interactions. Extension of such models to incorporate interconnected devices is a promising area for further investigation.

Verifying the security aspects of connected devices is a necessary part of their development. Connected devices react to inputs from other devices, transmit data to other devices and exchange information. The state space of unexpected inputs is large. Verifying the response of the GUI, of a connected device, to unexpected or crafted inputs is a challenging task. GUI models that help prune the state space of the GUI can be useful for modeling and verifying security aspects of a GUI-based software.

GUIs belong to the larger class of systems known as *Event-Driven Systems*. Model-based verification methods developed for GUIs may also be adapted to other event-driven systems such as electronic devices for home use, automobiles, and heavy machinery. These model-based methods can be used for testing event-driven systems in isolation and as connected devices including their security characteristics.

Model-based verification of GUIs has shown considerable maturity, growth, and research interest over the last decade. Continued development, investigation, and extension of model-based GUI testing methods is a necessary part of developing GUI-based software.

REFERENCES

[1] A.M. Memon, Developing testing techniques for event-driven pervasive computing applications, in: Proceedings of the OOPSLA 2004 Workshop on Building Software for Pervasive Computing (BSPC 2004), 2004.
[2] A.M. Memon, I. Banerjee, A. Nagarajan, What test Oracle should I use for effective GUI testing? in: Conference on Automated Software Engineering, 2003, pp. 164–173.
[3] J.H. Hicinbothom, W.W. Zachary, A tool for automatically generating transcripts of human–computer interaction, in: Proceedings of the Human Factors and Ergonomics Society 37th Annual Meeting, vol. 2, 1993, p. 1042.

[4] R.K. Shehady, D.P. Siewiorek, A method to automate user interface testing using variable finite state machines, in: Symposium on Fault-Tolerant Computing, 1997, p. 80.

[5] L. White, H. Almezen, Generating test cases for GUI responsibilities using complete interaction sequences, in: Symposium on Software Reliability Engineering, 2000, p. 110.

[6] F. Belli, Finite-state testing and analysis of graphical user interfaces, in: Symposium on Software Reliability Engineering, 2001, p. 34.

[7] A.M. Memon, Q. Xie, Studying the fault-detection effectiveness of GUI test cases for rapidly evolving software, IEEE Trans. Softw. Eng. 31 (2005) 884–896.

[8] X. Yuan, A.M. Memon, Generating event sequence-based test cases using GUI runtime state feedback. IEEE Trans. Softw. Eng. 36 (2010) 81–95, ISSN: 0098-5589. http://dx.doi.org/10.1109/TSE.2009.68.

[9] Q. Xie, A.M. Memon, Designing and comparing automated test oracles for GUI-based software applications, ACM Trans. Softw. Eng. Methodol. 16 (1) (2007) 1–36.

[10] A.C.R. Paivaa, J.C.P. Fariaa, R.F.A.M. Vidal, Towards the integration of visual and formal models for GUI testing, Electron. Notes Theor. Comput. Sci. 190 (2) (2007) 99–111.

[11] M. Risoldi, D. Buchs, A domain specific language and methodology for control systems GUI specification, verification and prototyping, in: IEEE Symposium on Visual Languages and Human-Centric Computing, IEEE, 2007, pp. 179–182. http://ieeexplore.ieee.org/document/4351345/.

[12] T.-H. Chang, T. Yeh, R.C. Miller, GUI testing using computer vision, in: Conference on Human Factors in Computing Systems, 2010, pp. 1535–1544.

[13] S. Esmelioglu, L. Apfelbaum, Automated test generation, execution, and reporting, in: Proceedings of Pacific Northwest Software Quality Conference, IEEE Press, 1997. http://citeseerx.ist.psu.edu/showciting;jsessionid=A91817740AE9B92444E9C47BA2D5A60D?cid=2060399.

[14] A. Memon, I. Banerjee, A. Nagarajan, GUI ripping: reverse engineering of graphical user interfaces for testing, in: Conference on Reverse Engineering, 2003, pp. 260–269.

[15] A.M. Memon, M.E. Pollack, M.L. Soffa, Hierarchical GUI test case generation using automated planning, IEEE Trans. Softw. Eng. 27 (2) (2001) 144–155.

[16] Q. Xie, A.M. Memon, Using a pilot study to derive a GUI model for automated testing, ACM Trans. Softw. Eng. Methodol. 18 (2) (2008) 1–33.

[17] D.J. Kasik, H.G. George, Toward automatic generation of novice user test scripts, in: Proceedings of the SIGCHI Conference on Human Factors in Computing Systems, ACM, New York, NY, 1996, pp. 244–251.

[18] X. Yuan, M.B. Cohen, A.M. Memon, GUI interaction testing: incorporating event context, in: IEEE Transactions on Software Engineering, 2010.

[19] I. Banerjee, B. Nguyen, V. Garousi, A. Memon, Graphical user interface (GUI) testing: systematic mapping and repository, Inf. Softw. Technol. 55 (2013) 1679–1694.

ABOUT THE AUTHOR

Ishan Banerjee obtained a Ph.D. in computer science from the University of Maryland, College Park in the area of model-based GUI testing. At present he works at VMware, USA. His research interests are in model-based testing of event-driven software and kernel-level memory resource management in a hypervisor.

CHAPTER THREE

Fault Localization Using Hybrid Static/Dynamic Analysis

E. Elsaka
University of Maryland, College Park, MD, United States

Contents

Abstract

With the increasing complexity of today's software, the software development process is becoming highly time and resource consuming. The increasing number of software configurations, input parameters, usage scenarios, supporting platforms, external dependencies, and versions plays an important role in expanding the costs of maintaining and repairing unforeseeable software faults. To repair software faults, developers spend considerable time in identifying the scenarios leading to those faults and root causing the problems.

While software debugging remains largely manual, it is not the case with software testing and verification. The goal of this research is to improve the software development process in general, and software debugging process in particular, by devising techniques and methods for automated software debugging, which leverage the advances in automatic test case generation and replay.

In this research, novel algorithms are devised to discover faulty execution paths in programs by utilizing already existing software test cases, which can be either

Advances in Computers, Volume 105
ISSN 0065-2458
http://dx.doi.org/10.1016/bs.adcom.2016.12.004

automatically or manually generated. The execution traces or, alternatively, the sequence covers of the failing test cases are extracted. Afterward, commonalities between these test case sequence covers are extracted, processed, analyzed, and then presented to the developers in the form of subsequences that may be causing the fault. The hypothesis is that code sequences that are shared between a number of faulty test cases for the same reason resemble the faulty execution path, and hence, the search space for the faulty execution path can be narrowed down by using a large number of test cases.

To achieve this goal, an efficient algorithm is implemented for finding common subsequences among a set of code sequence covers. Optimization techniques are devised to generate shorter and more logical sequence covers, and to select subsequences with high likelihood of containing the root cause among the set of all possible common subsequences. A hybrid static/dynamic analysis approach is designed to trace back the common subsequences from the end to the root cause.

1. INTRODUCTION

Software debugging is a main activity in the software development process. It is used extensively by software developers to localize faults, find sources of errors, and enhance software quality and performance in general. The most popular way to localize faults is by manual debugging, which is hard and time consuming [1]. In order for the developer to manually debug an application that contains an error, he/she has to first understand the way the application works and determine the root cause of the error by backtracking, navigating through the code dependencies, and possibly running the code multiple times and parsing the program logs in order to collect clues about the reasons of the error, so that the developer can finally identify the source of the error and fix it.

The need to understand the program functionality is very common, as there are many programmers who participate in the development phase. Therefore, the developer who works on fixing a specific bug may not necessarily have written the code, and thus, has to understand unfamiliar program parts. This task takes a considerable amount of effort and time [2]. Even after the developer becomes familiar with the code, figuring out the line(s) of code that produces the error is also a nontrivial task. The developer has to envision multiple scenarios (by exploring different possibilities of the input space) to check all the potentially error-causing execution paths. There has been some work in automating this step in the literature of software testing [3–9].

The final step, which is determining the source of the error (*fault localization*), is the hardest aspect of debugging [2] because it requires analyzing hundreds of lines to determine the error-causing subset. The developer has to track the program dependencies in the source code, and go through multiple dependency paths to know which are the ones that are exercised by the failing scenario.

Although software debugging remains largely manual, it is not the case with software testing. With recent advances in automatic software test case generation, new approaches use automatically generated test cases to facilitate software testing and detecting software bugs. There are different paradigms in the literature upon which automatic test case generation techniques are based. Some techniques are based on behavioral and interactional UML models [10–26]. Other techniques are based on structure UML models [27–30]. Also, there are some techniques that are based on other models such as Event Flow Graph model [31], Event Interaction Graph model [32], Feature model [33], and the Mathematical model [34]. All these approaches share the common goal of generating a large number of test cases for automatically detecting software bugs.

In this chapter, the advances achieved in software testing are leveraged to aid the process of automated software debugging. A novel approach for automated software debugging is developed, which is called *Disqover*, or debugging via *code sequence covers*. In this approach, automatically generated test cases are utilized to discover bugs and to help the developer find the source (lines of code) of those bugs. Sequences of lines of code, which are executed by these test cases, are recorded, analyzed, and output as a sequence of code statements (with dynamically observed values of variables) that cause the fault. A series of improvements are developed to the basic algorithm to enhance the output sequence to be more comprehensible, concise, and representative of the error execution scenario so that developers can achieve maximum utilization of the approach's output information.

The advantage of adopting a sequence-based approach is that finding error-causing code using the output in the form of code sequences is easier and more convenient for the developer than inspecting the code itself for the following reasons.

- Code sequences are examined in linear order. Developers do not need to track code dependencies and consider different paths through which the code can be executed.
- Code sequences are derived from execution traces, and hence capture runtime behavior as well.
- While generating code sequences, values of program variables are automatically extracted, so that the developer can examine them, and relate the variable assignments to the error.

2. MOTIVATING EXAMPLE

In this section, a debugging scenario is demonstrated using a bug in the open source Java application *Crossword Sage*.[a]

Crossword Sage is a tool for creating professional-looking crosswords with powerful word suggestion capabilities. It can be used to build, load, and save crosswords. It can suggest words for adding to the crosswords and allows the crosswords builder to give clues for them. Furthermore, in addition to building crosswords, it allows users to load prebuilt crosswords and solve them. Crossword Sage project consists of 3072 lines of code, 34 classes, and 238 methods.

In order for the user to create a new crossword puzzle, he/she needs to click on the File menu and choose the New Crossword menu item. Then, the application asks the user to input the size of the puzzle through a dialog box. When the user inputs a numeric number between 2 and 20, the application creates an empty Grid to allow the user to start building his/her crossword puzzle.

Normally, if the user enters a nonnumeric value as the size of the puzzle, an error dialog box should appear that says wrong input value and asks the user to enter another input value. However, in this application when the user enters a nonnumeric value in the dialog box, the application crashes with a *NumberFormatException*.

Using the most popular debugging method, which is the manual debugging, the developer may follow the following steps in order to locate the source of the error and fix it.

- Initially, the developer locates the line in the source code that is responsible of throwing the exception. In the example, it is line number 33 in the Grid class (setLayout(new GridLayout(Integer.parseInt(cw.getHeight()), Integer.parseInt(cw.getWidth())))).
- Then, the developer should go to this line to investigate the line and try to extract any clues about the reason of the exception.
- From the line, the developer can conclude that the width or the height of the "cw" object might not have been initialized correctly. So, when the Integer.parseInt() function parses the value of any of them, it leads to the NumberFormatException. Now, the user needs to locate where the height and the width of the "cw" object have been firstly initialized.

---

[a] http://crosswordsage.sourceforge.net.

- Furthermore, the developer may put a break point at this line to figure out the values of the width and height variables to make sure they are not correctly set as numeric values and run the program once to validate this assumption.
- Using the "Find References" feature available on some IDEs, the developer can find the methods calling the method containing the line 33. There are four choices. The developer may need to check each of them to see if they have been on the execution path of that particular error.
- The developer may need to run the program once more to see which of the options is on the execution path. He/she may also need to add more debugging information. It will turn out that line 40 in the CrosswordCompiler class is the one calling the line 33 in the Grid class, and passing the parameter values.
- This line shows that a new instance of the Grid is created with the cw object passed as a parameter which is created in the previous line with the width and height variables that are passed as CrosswordCompiler constructor parameters.
- Also, the developer may again put a break point at this location and run the program again to test the values of the width and height variables.
- The developer also may verify the creation of the cw object by going to the Crossword class which shows that the Crossword constructor initializes the width and the height of the object using the constructor parameters and it assumes that valid values are passed.
- By repeating the procedure above, the developer can find that line 226 in the MainScreen class is the line responsible of creating the CrosswordCompiler object.
- The developer can see that the initialization of the CrosswordCompiler parameters is carried out through the "reply" variable. This variable is initialized in the previous line using an input from a dialog box and no check is made regarding the type of the reply variable.
- Again the developer may put a break point at this location and run the program again with different input values to initialize the reply variable and see the effect of these values on the width and height variables.
- At this point the developer will discover that a check is needed to verify that the values of the reply string are numeric, or otherwise the program cannot proceed.

As can be seen, using manual debugging, the user has to navigate to the source code many times in order to analyze the code and figure out the cause of the error. Furthermore, the user may run the program again to find out the values that cause the failure.

On the contrary, using Disqover, the user does not need to either navigate to the source code nor run the program again. Fig. 1 shows the resulting subsequence from applying developed approach to the execution traces of a set of test cases which fail by producing the NumberFormatException at the same line of code.

In order for the developer to find the source of the error using developed approach, the following activities will take place:

- In Fig. 1, the last highlighted line is the line (setLayout(new GridLayout (Integer.parseInt(cw.getHeight()), Integer.parseInt(cw.getWidth())));). This line is the line that throws the NumberFormatException. From this line, the developer can conclude that this exception results from applying the Integer.parseInt() function to a nonnumeric value.

- This nonnumeric value may be assigned to either the *height* or the *width* variables of the *cw* object (because the Integer.parseInt() appears twice in the line).

- Now, the developer can go backward in the subsequence to figure out where these two variables get assigned.

- The developer can see that the *cw* object comes from the method parameter as shown in line (public Grid(Crossword cw)).

- Since this method represents a constructor, there should be a line in the sequence that creates new object from the Grid class and passes the Crossword object as a parameter as can be seen at the line (grid = new Grid(cw)).

- By going backward, the developer can see that the Crossword object *cw* is created at the line (cw = new Crossword(width,height);) and the width and the height are passed as parameters.

- These width and height variables are passed to the function through the CrosswordCompiler constructor arguments at line (public CrosswordCompiler(String width, String height)).

- Finally, by going backward at crosswordsage.MainScreen class, the developer can see that these parameters are passed as arguments when creating a new instance of crosswordsage.CrosswordCompiler at line (cc = new CrosswordCompiler(reply, reply)) and these arguments are both initialized by the variable *reply* which takes string values in line (String reply = jOptionPane.showInputDialog(null, "Please enter grid size (2 - 20)...", null);).

As it can be seen from the example, the developer does not need to refer to the source code because all the required information exists in the resulted

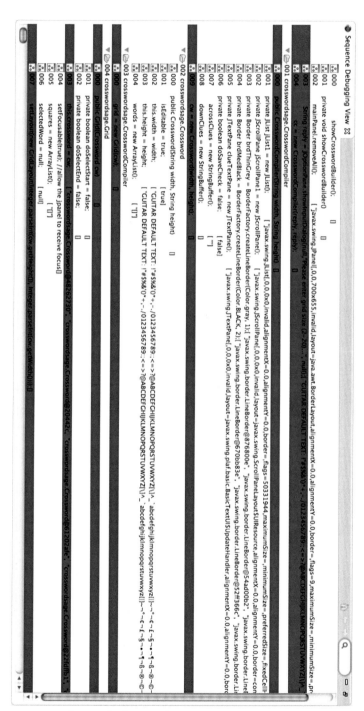

Fig. 1 A sequence that results from applying developed approach on the seeded fault in Crossword Sage application.

subsequence. Furthermore, the values that are assigned to the variables during the test cases execution are also available for the developer's convenience.

3. EXISTING APPROACHES

In this section, the related work to the research in the area of automated software debugging is reviewed. First, the early research that has been done in this field, which is a set of techniques called *program slicing* is presented. Second, *differential debugging* techniques are presented. These techniques narrow down the set of possible statements causing an error using the differences between either the working and nonworking software versions or passed and failed test cases. Third, a technique that is based on failed test cases only is discussed. Fourth, approaches based on machine learning and data mining techniques and model-based approaches are discussed. Finally, some related work about automated performance debugging are presented.

3.1 Slicing

Research in the area of automated debugging started a long time ago by Weiser [35, 36], who proposed *program slicing*. Slicing defines all the statements that can affect a variable in a program. Therefore, given a variable v in a program P, slice S contains all the statement in P that may affect the value of v. The main idea is that if the statement that contains the variable v is erroneous, the source of this error can be in slice S. Slicing is calculated either statically [35, 36] by finding the relevant statement according to data and control dependencies or dynamically [37] by benefiting from information collected during the program execution. Although dynamic slicing and its variations [38–41] potentially reduce the size of the slices and improve debugging, the size of the slices is still fairly large and slicing techniques are rarely used in practice. The slice, which is the output of the slicing algorithm, is a reduced version of the original program. It only contains the statements that affect the value of the output and has the same behavior as the original program. Therefore, the debugger still has to run the reduced program again and manually detect the source of the error. On the contrary, Disqover provides sequences of statements that take place when running the failed test cases with each statement associated with the possible variable values. Therefore, the debugger can easily find the source of the error by backtracking these sequences.

3.2 Differential Techniques

3.2.1 Techniques Based on Working and Nonworking Program Versions

This category assumes that there are at least two versions of the program, a working version and a nonworking one. This means that running a test case passes in one version and does not in the other one. Therefore, a source of an error can be found by computing the difference between the working and nonworking versions. One approach of this category is *regression containment* [42]. It isolates the changes that cause the error by defining the set of changes that have been done between the working and nonworking (that is not passing the test) program editions. Since there can be multiple changes, it encapsulates the related changes together in identifiable objects called mods and orders them in chronological order (i.e., by the order they were introduced to the original program). The mods are removed from the nonworking edition in reverse chronological order either linearly (one by one) or binary until the test passes. The last mod that has been removed is the mod that is responsible of the test failure. This method works effectively if one change is causing the error, but not a combination of changes. Also, while a change may contain hundred or even thousands of lines of code, only a few lines may be responsible of the error. Finally, the chronological order of changes may not always be available or easily obtained.

Delta debugging (DD) [24] is proposed to address the limitations of regression containment. It is similar to the regression containment technique in relying on the existence of working and nonworking versions of the software and investigating the set of changes between the two versions. Assuming that a set S contains all the changes that have been done between the passing and failing versions, if S contains one change, this means that the source of the error is in S. Otherwise, S is partitioned into two sets S_1 and S_2, and each set is tested separately. If either of S_1 or S_2 produces the failure, this means that S_1 or S_2, respectively, contains the source of the error, and it is subject to more binary partitioning. If both of them pass, this means that the source of the error comes from a combination of them. Therefore, the combination of the two sets is partitioned in different ways until the minimal combination of changes is identified. This divide-and-conquer algorithm takes care of interference (i.e., a combination of changes is responsible of the error) and granularity (a single change may encompass hundreds of lines of code but a small subset of it may be responsible of the error) which are not addressed in the regression containment technique. DD not only minimizes the difference between two program versions but also the differences between two inputs where one input is correctly run by the program and the other one is failed to be run as proposed in Ref. [25].

Other variations of DD have been proposed to overcome its limitations such as *Hierarchical Delta Debugging (HDD)* and *Iterative Delta Debugging (IDD)* [1]. Although, DD effectively identifies the source of the error, it is only applicable with independent change list in which each change in the list is independent of the other changes, e.g., a change containing a for loop and another containing its body form dependent changes, while two for loops are independent. This constraint makes DD works poorly with the data that has hierarchical structure-like object-oriented programs and XML input files. Therefore, HDD was proposed to overcome this limitation by applying the DD algorithm on each level of the algorithm's input starting from coarsest to the finest levels. IDD finds an older program version, among the existing versions, in which a test case passes but fails in the current version. In some cases, a test case may not be applicable to older versions. Therefore, IDD successively uses DD to apply the necessary changes from the newer version to an older version until it finds an older version that allows a test case to run. IDD starts with the current version P_c (which fails the test case t). It successively goes back and checks the older versions P_{o^i}. If the output of P_{o^i} for running t matches the output of P_c, IDD skips this version and proceeds with $P_{o^{i-1}}$ version. If the output of P_{o^i} is undetermined, DD is applied between the two versions P_c and P_{o^i}, and another version is produced called P'_{o^i} which behaves the same as P_c with the test case t. This process proceeds until either the version that passes t is found or there is no more older versions.

All these techniques rely on the existence of either working and non-working versions of the program under test or passing and failing inputs. This assumption is not true in most cases because of either the absence of older program versions or the absence of another version that allows the test case to run. Also, extracting the changes between two program versions and applying parts of these changes to the working version are very time consuming because of the execution time required to run multiple combinations of these changes especially for large applications, and it also cannot be done in parallel because the run at one iteration depends on the output of the run at the previous iteration. Furthermore, applying part of the changes to the working version may not always result in an executable version. Moreover, the output of all the previous techniques is a set of lines without any further information. Finally, those approaches operate on static versions of the programs and do not incorporate runtime information back into the debugging output. Conversely, Disqover just relies on the current version of the program. Also, it does not need to worry about changing the source code or generating executable versions of the program. Lastly, it uses the dynamic execution trace of the program and generates sequences of statements that take place when running the failed test cases with each statement associated with the possible variable values.

3.2.2 Techniques Based on Passed and Failed Test Cases

The idea of the second category is based on finding at least one passing test case that is approximately similar to a failing one and extracting the difference between the execution of the test cases. There are multiple types of test case-based automated debugging techniques such as approaches based on *path profiles* [43], *counter examples* [44, 45], *statement coverage* [46, 47], *statement mutants* [48], *predicate values* [49, 50], and *program states* [51, 52]. These approaches differ from each other in the type of information that they rely on to define the characteristics of the program execution.

Approaches based on path profiles [43] identify the program paths that are explored during the passed and the failed test cases by instrumenting the program during the test case execution. Then it finds the differences between the two sets of paths. In other words, it defines the paths that are present during the execution of the passed test cases and are not present during the execution of the failed test cases S_p and visa versa S_f. Finally, it calculates the shortest prefixes that appear in all the paths of S_p and do not appear in all the paths of S_f. These prefixes present the critical portions of the code that the programmer should investigate to define the source of the error.

Approaches based on counter examples [44, 45], use the trace reports that result from model checking tools for passing and failing test cases. Then, it takes the differences between the two trace reports. For each error, it compares one error trace with one correct trace.

Approaches based on statement coverage [47, 53] use visualization tools to represent the suspicious code statements. These tools use different techniques to color the program statements according to their participation in the test case execution. Ruthruff *et al.* [53] uses one color to mark the statements that exist in the dynamic slices of the failed test cases and do not exist in the dynamic slices of the passed test cases. These statements most probably contain the source of the fault. At the same time, it uses another color to color the statements that exist in the dynamic slices of the execution of all the test cases. These statements less likely contain the source of the error.

Jones *et al.* [47] colors the statements according to their percentage of participation in running the test cases. So, the statements that participate in the execution of more failed test cases than passed test cases are colored with more reddish color. On the other hand, the statements that participate in the execution of more passed test cases than failed test cases are colored with more greenish color. The statements that have the same percentage of participation are colored with yellow color. Also, Wong *et al.* [54] define the suspiciousness of each statement based on the relationship between its coverage and the execution results (failed/passed) of test cases. This is done by calculating the crosstab of each statement in which the columns represent the coverage information (covered/not covered) and the rows represent the execution results information (failed/passed). Furthermore, Naish *et al.* [46] calculate the suspiciousness of a statement according to the following formula:

$$O^p = a_{ef} - \frac{a_{ep}}{P+1},$$

where a_{ef} is the number of failed test cases that execute s, a_{ep} is the number of passed test cases that execute s, and P is the total number of passed test cases. They expect that buggy statements have high a_{ef} and low a_{ep}, which leads to a high suspiciousness score. Therefore, statement with the highest suspiciousness score are most likely to be buggy.

One of the most recent and effective techniques is given in Ref. [48]. It creates mutants for each statements according to different characteristics. To create a mutant for a statement, it should be hit by a failed test case. Finally, they calculate the suspiciousness of a statement according to the following formula:

$$suspiciousness(e) = \frac{1}{|mut(s)|} \sum_{m \in mut(s)} \left(\frac{|f_p(s) \cap p_m|}{|f_p|} - \alpha \frac{|p_p(s) \cap f_m|}{|p_p|} \right),$$

where $mut(s)$ is the number of mutants that are generated for a statement s, $\dfrac{|f_p(s) \cap p_m|}{|f_p|}$ is the proportion of tests that failed on P but now pass on a mutant m that mutates s over tests that failed on P, $\dfrac{|p_p(s) \cap f_m|}{|p_p|}$ is the proportion of tests that passed on P but now fail on a mutant m that mutates s over tests that passed on P, and α as

$$\alpha = \frac{f2p}{|mut(P)| \cdot |f_p|} \cdot \frac{|mut(P)| \cdot |p_p|}{|p2f|},$$

where $f2p$ and $p2f$ are the number of test result changes from failure to pass and vice versa between before and after all mutants of P, $mut(P)$ is the number of mutants that are generated for all the statements of P. Their hypothesis is that mutating a faulty statement will either keep the program faulty or fix the program partially. At the same time, mutating a correct statement is more likely introduce a new fault.

Approaches based on predicate values [49, 50] associate bugs in the program with predicates that are instrumented during the execution of the program. The algorithm in Ref. [49] computes two probabilities for each predicate P. *Failure(P)*, which is the probability of P being true implies failure, and *Context(P)*, which is the probability of executing P may produce failure. Then, it discards the predicates that have *Failure(P) − Context(P)* ≤ 0. Finally, it prioritizes the remaining predicates based on their score. On the other hand, the algorithm in Ref. [50] computes the probability of a predicate P is evaluated to true in each run as $\pi(p) = n(t)/(n(t) + n(f))$ where $n(t)$ is the number of times that P is evaluated to true in a specific run and $n(f)$ is the number of times that P is evaluated to false. Then, it correlates a predicate to a bug if its distribution during the failed test cases is significantly different from that in successful test cases.

Zeller [51] and Cleve *et al.* [52] propose approaches based on the differences between the program states (which consists the variables and their values at particular point during the program execution) during the passed and failed program executions.

The problem with these techniques is that the number of lines of code that they identify for inspection by the developer can still be high because it is not always possible to find close enough failing and passing test cases. Furthermore, the developer still needs to inspect the source code to understand the context of the suggested statements. Also, some techniques like [48] takes too much time in order to calculate the statements suspiciousness.

3.3 Techniques Based on Failed Test Cases

Zhang *et al.* [55] propose a fault localization technique that is based on failing test cases only. Their hypothesis is that the more faulty runs that go through a program entity (e.g., statement), the more likely this entity can lead to the failure. They use the following formula to calculate the suspiciousness of a statement:

$$suspiciousness(e) = \frac{\sum_{c \in D}[c(Y(c) - Y(0))] \times c_{max} / \sum_{c \in D} c^2}{\sqrt{\sum_{c \in D}(Y(c) - Y(0))^2 - \left(\sum_{c \in D}[c(Y(c) - Y(0))]\right)^2 / \sum_{c \in D} c^2}},$$

where c is the number of times in which a test case executes e, $Y(c)$ is the number of test cases that executes e c times, and $Y(0)$ is the number of test cases that never execute e. This technique still has the same problems of the techniques that are discussed in Section 3.2.2 because it provides the developer with a list of ranked statements.

3.4 Machine Learning-Based Approaches

A number of research studies propose machine learning and data mining methods for fault localization. Wong and Qi [56] propose an approach based on back-propagation (BP) neural networks for fault localization. It utilizes the statement coverage information for passing and failing test cases to train a BP neural network in which the network learns the relationship between the coverage and the success or failure of test cases. Then it computes the suspiciousness of the program statement by including this statement in a virtual test case and using the virtual test case as an input to the BP network. Furthermore, Wong *et al.* [57] use the same algorithm that is proposed by Wong and Qi [56] but using RBF (radial basis function) networks to overcome the limitations of BP neural network such as network paralysis (network learning stops) and local optimization.

Briand *et al.* [58] analyze test case specifications in terms of their input and output to identify distinct conditions of failure using C4.5 decision trees. Each path in this type of trees represents a rule for distinct failure condition with a probability prediction for distinct failure. The statement coverage for the passed and failed test cases are used for ranking failure conditions. Then the ranking of failure conditions is used for the final ranking of the statements that should be examined to detect the source of a failure.

Brun *et al.* [59] propose a machine learning approach based on support vector machines or decision trees. This approach consists of two phases: training and classification phases. The training phase builds a model using previously known errors and program properties (e.g., program variables). The input to this phase is two program versions, one has one fault and the other does not have that fault. The properties of each version are extracted and classified to fault revealing, which exist in the faulty version and do not exist in the nonfaulty one and nonfault revealing, which exist in both versions. The classification phase applies the training model to the set of properties that are specified by the user and outputs the set of properties that are more likely related to the error ordered by their likelihood of being fault revealing.

Nessa *et al.* [60] compute a set of subsequences of length N (N-grams) from the traces of test cases execution. In order to define these N-grams, they identify the execution blocks by constructing Execution Sequence Graph. In this graph, the vertices represent the lines of code and the edges represent the consecutive relationship between the lines. An edge exists between two vertices if they are executed consecutively in at least one test case. This definition of blocks reduces the size of the trace and helps in defining possible branches. Using these blocks, all possible N-grams of lengths 1 to N are generated. Then, the number of occurrences of each N-gram is calculated in the failed test cases and the ones that are greater than a specified threshold are selected. Finally, the chosen N-gram subsequences are ordered based on their calculated conditional probabilities that a given test case is failed because the appearance of a specific N-gram.

Cellier *et al.* [61] propose a data mining method to identify rules between the statement execution and test case failure based on association rules and formal concept analysis (FCA). First, they build the trace context in which the objects are the execution traces of the test cases, and the attributes are the lines of the program and if the test case pass or fail. Second, they generate the association rules that are strongly related to the failure and specify a minimum threshold. Third, they define the relation between the defined rules using the rule context and rule lattice. Finally, to detect the fault, the rule lattice is investigated bottom up in order to investigate the more specific rules first, then the more general ones.

None of these approaches ensures that the statement that contains the source of the error will exist in the resulting suggested statements. Furthermore, the user still needs to examine the source code to define the source of the error using the clues (list of statements, which are ordered according of their suspiciousness) that are reported by these approaches.

3.5 Model-Based Approaches

Some research studies are proposed to analyze the relationship between the failures and the faults or between the source and the failure. Wotawa *et al.* [62] propose a model-based approach that exploits the program variable dependencies, the control flow, and the whole semantics of the program. The model behavior is extracted from the test cases in terms of their input and output. For searching for the bug locations when a test case contradicts with the model, each program statement is assumed to be correct or incorrect by default, then this assumption is revised during the debugging process until identifying the cause of the error. Mateis *et al.* [63] propose a model-based approach for a subset of features of Java programs such as classes, methods, assignments, conditionals, and while-loop. The program is statically compiled to a model, which can be divided into two parts: the structural part and the behavioral part. The structural part presents the program components and the connectivity relations between them. The behavioral part, which helps in defining the faulty statements, represents the behavior of these components using a logic-based language. Mayer *et al.* [64, 65] extended this model-based approach to handle the unstructured control flows of Java programs such as exceptions, recursive method calls, return, and jump statements.

Furthermore, DeMillo *et al.* [66] propose a model-based approach that describes the relationship between the failure and the faults. The model consists of failure modes and failure types. Failure modes describe the different symptoms of the program failure. Using these failure modes a program failure is categorized. Failure types describe the nature of the failures. In order to localize the failure, the following steps are followed. First, the failure mode is identified. Then using the model, which describes the relations between the modes and the types, the type of the failure is identified. Finally, using heuristics based on dynamic instrumentation and testing information, the search domain is reduced for predicting possible faulty statements.

Model-based approaches are difficult to apply on real applications because it is extremely hard or impossible to generate a model that accommodates all program behaviors, which makes the model incomplete.

3.6 Performance Debugging

Some approaches have been proposed also for debugging software performance. These approaches focus on defining the system bottlenecks that result from I/O operations, CPU, or memory consumption. One of these approaches is given in Ref. [67], which is an approach for summarizing the execution profiles of large systems and identifying overlaps between these summaries. Using a search tool over the summaries, the system bottlenecks can be identified. Also, Srinivas and Srinivasan [68] propose an approach that uses *thresholding* and *filtering* to define a small set of costly methods invocations. Thresholding chooses only the components that exceed the user-defined threshold and filtering filters out the user-defined components. Sevitsky *et al.* [69] provide a visualization tool called Jinsight EX that allows the user to choose the most valuable information that should be included during performance analysis. This tool is used to define Java applications bottlenecks. Han *et al.* [70] propose StackMine, a tool for effectively identifying the cause of performance bugs that are reported through the execution traces of a huge number of users. It applies mining algorithms on these execution traces to define the most costly subsequences of function calls that account for a nontrivial waiting time, then it identifies the signature that causes this delay. Altman *et al.* [71] focus on identifying the cause of the idle time in server applications by analyzing their states of idleness during the execution time using WAIT tool.

4. MODELING DISQOVER

In this section, Disqover, an automated debugging approach is discussed. Disqover is applicable to all types of softwares. The section starts by stating some basic definitions, then it discusses Disqover in detail in the following sections.

Definition 1. (Test case) Given a software S, a test case is a set of inputs i_1, i_2, ..., i_n that satisfy a set of preconditions, along with a set of expected outputs o_1, o_2, ..., o_m that satisfy a set of postconditions. When i_1, i_2, ..., i_n are given to software S, S should produce o_1, o_2, ..., o_m in order for the test case to pass.

Definition 2. (Passing/failing test case) Given a software S and a test case t, t passes if S runs t to completion correctly, producing the expected output, and t fails if t causes S to produce an unexpected output during the execution of t.

In the approach, the failing test cases that fail for the same reason (i.e., that find the same type of error or the unexpected output at the same statement) are grouped together under the same *test cases group*. Test case groups enable debugging applications that have multiple errors at the same time.

Definition 3. (Test cases group) A test cases group is a set that contains one or more test cases that fail at the same location, producing the same type of error or unexpected output.

Furthermore, two types of statements that are essential for such type of automated debugging are defined, *failure statement* and *root cause subsequence*.

Definition 4. (Failure statement) It is the statement where the unexpected output is detected. The failure can also take the form of an application error.

It is noticed that neither the failure statement nor its function call stack trace are necessarily responsible for the unexpected output, and hence, the need for identifying the root cause becomes apparent, which is the bulk of the software debugging process, and the objective of Disqover.

Definition 5. (Root cause subsequence) It is a subsequence of statements that is the main reason for the unexpected output. This subsequence may consist of a single or multiple statements. Fixing this subsequence prevents the unexpected output from being produced.

In this approach, the commonalities between multiple test cases which fail for the same reason (i.e., from the test case group) are extracted. By using more than one failing test case, the subsequence responsible for the error is narrowed down, by eliminating irrelevant statements that are not shared between the execution traces of all the test cases.

A straightforward way for implementing the above observation is by finding a simple set intersection of the statements shared by test cases in a group (code coverage intersection). However, this approach is inadequate, as it returns an unordered set of statement with no relationship between them. Therefore, the basic idea of the developed approach is to extract the common subsequence among the failing test cases sequence covers. Using sequence covers as opposed to code coverage intersection has a number of advantages. Tracing the common subsequence back starting from the failure statement makes the debugging process as simple as a linear scan, as opposed to exploring the highly interconnected program dependency graph to trace back an application error. Furthermore, exploiting the fact that the program statements execute in sequence can reduce the number of statements reported, because in this case, not only the statements that are just shared between the sequences will be considered, but also these statements must be executed in the same order. The existence of this additional restriction further decreases the number of the resulting statements that the developer needs to consider at a time.

Below a motivating application is presented for using sequence covers for automated debugging, as opposed to using code coverage intersection, but first, these both terms are defined.

Definition 6. (Test case code coverage $C(t)$) Given a test case t, the test case code coverage $C(t)$ is a set of statements that are executed during the execution of t.

Definition 7. (Test case sequence cover $S(t)$) Given a test case t, a sequence cover, $S(t)$, is the *ordered list* of statements that are executed during the execution of t according to their execution order.

4.1 Motivating Example

Consider the code snippet listed in Fig. 2, which has the statements s_1, s_2, s_3, s_4, and s_5 (the *if* and the *for* statements are excluded from the sequence for simplicity). It can also execute two test cases t_1 and t_2, which are from the same test case group. t_1 executes the statements s_1, s_3, s_4, s_5 in the following order $s_1 \rightarrow s_3 \rightarrow s_4 \rightarrow s_5$ and t_2 executes the statements s_2, s_3, s_4, s_5 in the following order $s_2 \rightarrow s_5 \rightarrow s_3 \rightarrow s_4$. The two test cases execute each statement only once. In this case, the code coverage set $C(t_1)$ is $\{s_1, s_3, s_4, s_5\}$ and the code coverage set $C(t_2)$ is $\{s_2, s_3, s_4, s_5\}$. Therefore, the statements that result from applying the code coverage intersection technique are (s_3, s_4, s_5). On the other hand, if the order of statement execution is utilized, it can be said that either the subsequence s_3, s_4 or the subsequence s_5 is responsible of the error because in the first test case, s_5 appears before s_3, s_4 and in the second it appears after them. Therefore, s_5 can be inspected in isolation of s_3 and s_4 by the developer, which minimizes the number of statements to consider at a time, and minimizes the number of interactions and dependencies that the developer needs to keep track of while tracing back the statements. In this case, the execution trace of each test case is generated as a sequence of statements, and the common *ordered* statements between all the test cases are extracted.

```
if (t1) s1;

if (t2) s2;

for (i in 0,1) {

    if(t1 && i=0 || t2 && i=1) {

    s3; s4; }

    if(t1 && i=1 || t2 && i=0) s5;

}
```

Fig. 2 Example program.

4.2 The Disqover Approach

Now, Disqover, an automated debugging approach is discussed. Disqover takes as an input the test suite and the source code of the application under test (AUT) and outputs the detected faults with their recommended code subsequence that lead to the source of the fault.

Disqover consists of five steps:

1. The Execution Trace & Logs Extraction, which extracts the test cases execution traces and the test cases execution logs. The execution traces present the order of the statements that are touched during the execution of the test cases. The execution logs present the output of each test case, i.e., whether it passed or failed.
2. Test cases partitioning, which groups the test cases according to the type and the location of the faults caught by the test cases execution. It takes as an input the test cases execution logs and outputs test case groups. Each group has the test cases that are failed for the same fault (exception, error, or false assertion) type at the same location in the source code. In addition, it outputs an additional group for all the passed test cases.
3. Common subsequence extraction, which extracts a common subsequence of lines found in the trace of the failing test cases.
4. Hybrid dynamic/static analysis, which uses both static information coming from code dependency analysis and dynamic information coming from the common subsequence from the previous step, to provide the dependency of the failed line within the common subsequence. It takes as input the common subsequence and outputs a final subsequence. This subsequence explains the fault since it contains only the lines that affect the failed line.
5. Remote Debugging, which provides the values of the variables that included in the subsequence that explains the fault.

In the following sections, each step is discussed in more details.

4.2.1 The Execution Trace & Logs Extraction

To analyze the failed test cases, the test case execution trace and execution log are captured. Test case execution trace presents which statements where touched during the test case execution. Since we care about the order of execution of the statements in addition to the statements themselves, this order is captured as well. Test case execution log presents the output of the test case (e.g., whether it passes or fails). To extract the test cases execution trace, a code instrumentation tool, Cobertura [72], is modified to achieve this task. Cobertura is an open source Java tool that calculates the percentage of code accessed by test cases. It instruments Java byte-code after program compilation. It can generate either HTML or XML reports. Each line is represented by package name, class name, method name, line number, and the number of hits during running the test case. In this research, Cobertura source code is modified so that it can output a report of the program execution trace in the form of a sequence of program lines that are touched during replaying the test case.

4.2.2 Test Cases Partitioning

In the partitioning step, the test cases are partitioned into groups. Each group has test cases that fail for the same reason. In other words, all the test cases that belong to the same group throw the same type of exception at the same location. This step takes as an input the logs of the test cases that result from executing the test cases. According to the type of the error and the location of this error in the source code, the test cases are grouped together. At the same time, all the passed test cases are grouped together to compare them to the test oracle in order to detect more faults. Fig. 3 shows an example of an HTML-based output of the partitioning step, partitioning the test cases of one of GUI applications, Crossword Sage, into groups according to the two types of errors found by running those test cases: NullPointerException, and NumberFormatException, along with the number of test cases relevant to each error, and a hyperlink to the detail pages explaining the reasons of those failures.

4.3 Common Subsequences Extraction

In this section the algorithm for finding code sequence coverage intersection is discussed in detail. The goal of the algorithm is to detect subsequences of statements that appear in all the test cases in the same order, and at the same time, not necessarily consecutively, i.e., they can have arbitrary gaps between them. For example, assuming the three execution traces in Fig. 3 are obtained, the algorithm is needed to detect that the subsequence (a, b, a) is the one that is common between them. Applying the longest common subsequences, LCS, algorithm is not suitable in this research as it outputs the longest common subsequence only, which may not contain the root

Application   : Crossword Sage
Number of test cases : 347
Number of faults   : 2

Exception	Location	Number of test cases	
java.lang.NullPointerException	crosswordsage.Grid at line 33	169	Details
java.lang.NumberFormatException	crosswordsage.Grid at line 33	41	Details

Fig. 3 Partitioning output.

cause of the error, as it is just one of the possible subsequences among all the common subsequences.

In this section the approach for finding all the common subsequences is discussed, and in Section 4.3.4, how to rank the subsequences according to their importance is shown so that the subsequence with the highest rank is outputted according to that criteria.

To enumerate all the possible common subsequences between a set of sequences, the steps outlined below are followed.

4.3.1 Applying Code Coverage Intersection

As an initial step, all the code coverage sets of the test cases are intersected to get the set of statements that are common between them. Clearly, the common subsequences must be composed of statements in that intersection only. This set is denoted as $C = C(t_1) \cap C(t_2)$....

4.3.2 Constructing the Common Subsequences Graph

The problem of generating all common subsequences among a set of sequences is difficult because there is an exponential number of combinations that can be considered in order to construct the common subsequence. If a statement appears multiple times in each sequence, say $n_1, \ldots, n_m$ times, then there are $O(\prod_i n_i)$ ways to construct smaller subsequences recursively out of the original ones to continue finding the common subsequences among them and so on. In this section, how to model that problem is discussed using the *common subsequences graph*, and how to compute the common subsequences efficiently by only considering meaningful combinations, because not all of the possible combinations can make it to the final common subsequences.

Since each statement can occur multiple times in each sequence cover, a particular combination of occurrences of a statement is defined in all sequence covers to be an *instance* of that statement, as it can possibly contribute to a common subsequence. For example, in Fig. 4,b has only one possible instance of occurrence: $(2, 3, 2)$, which means that b occurs at position 2 in $S(t_1)$, position 3 at $S(t_2)$, and position 2 at $S(t_3)$. However, a has *eight* possible

$$S(t_1) = a\ b\ a\ c$$

$$S(t_2) = c\ a\ b\ a$$

$$S(t_3) = a\ b\ d\ a$$

Fig. 4 Sequence covers of three test cases.

instances, since it occurs in $S(t_1)$ at positions 1, 3, in $S(t_2)$ at positions 2, 4, and in $S(t_3)$ at positions 1, 4. Therefore, a's possible combinations are (1, 2, 1), (1, 2, 4), (1, 4, 1), ...

Now that the instances of occurrences for each statement are defined, a common subsequence is a sequence of instances ($inst_1$, $inst_2$, ..., $inst_n$) such that all positions in $inst_i$ are *strictly less than* their corresponding positions in $inst_{i+1}$, for all $1 \leq i < n$.

Definition 8. (Operator $<$) Given two instances $inst_i$ and $inst_j$, $inst_i < inst_j$ if and only if all the positions in $inst_i$ are less than their corresponding positions in $inst_j$.

Likewise, $>$ is defined over pairs of instances, $inst_i$ and $inst_j$ using their corresponding positions.

Example 1. It consider the instance of a's occurrence $inst_1 = (1, 2, 4)$ and the instance of b's occurrence $inst_2 = (2, 3, 2)$. A common subsequence *cannot* consist of $inst_1$ followed by $inst_2$, because $inst_1 \nless inst_2$, because at the third place, a occurs at position 4 while b occurs at position 2, which means that a precedes b in all the test case sequences, but not in the third, where b precedes a, which means that ($inst_1$, $inst_2$) is not a valid common subsequence. On the other hand, if we consider $inst_1$ as the instance (1, 2, 1), then ($inst_1$, $inst_2$) becomes a valid common subsequence, because $inst_1 < inst_2$, where for every position in $inst_1$, its corresponding position in $inst_2$ is strictly greater than it, which means that a precedes b in all test cases.

The naive way for generating the common subsequences using the instances is by generating all possible instances ($inst_1$, $inst_2$, ...) for all statements and finding which of them follows the others, i.e., $inst_i < inst_j$.

This approach has a number of disadvantages:

1. It is quadratic in the number of instances, which is exponential in the number of test cases to begin with. So, it is very inefficient.

2. This approach may result in redundant common subsequences. For example, consider the instances $inst_1 = (1, 2, 1)$, representing a, and $inst_2 = (2, 3, 2)$, representing b, and $inst_3 = (3, 4, 4)$, representing another occurrence of a. An approach that blindly constructs common subsequences if the positions are strictly increasing will generate both the common subsequences ($inst_1$, $inst_2$, $inst_3$), i.e., aba, and ($inst_1$, $inst_3$), i.e., aa, because both follow the strictly increasing position criteria. However, a wiser approach should generate ($inst_1$, $inst_2$, $inst_3$) only, as ($inst_1$, $inst_3$) is already a subset of it.

3. This approach requires enumerating all the possible instances, even if we are not going to use them. For example, once we generate the instance $inst_1 = (1, 2, 1)$ for a, there is no need to generate $inst_2 = (1, 4, 1)$ for a, as $inst_2$ cannot appear with $inst_1$ in any common subsequence, and hence

we can save a lot of the exponential time complexity involved in generating *all possible instances.*

As it can be seen, it is inefficient to use an enumeration-based approach. In the experimental evaluation, this approach was evaluated as a baseline; however, it failed to find the common subsequences as it resulted in an out of memory exception due to its high memory requirements.

To make this process more scalable, an algorithm that generates the instances *on demand* and *avoids constructing redundant subsequences* during the common subsequence building time is developed. The algorithm is based on constructing a graph of instances, where nodes of the graph represent instances, and an edge from instance $inst_i$ to $inst_j$ means that $inst_i > inst_j$ *and* there is no other $inst_k$ such that $inst_i > inst_k$ and $inst_k > inst_j$, i.e., there is no intermediate instance that can appear in the common subsequence between $inst_i$ and $inst_j$, and hence, edges of the graph are constructed between nodes that represent instances that *directly* follow each other.

In order to generate the instances on demand, the least instance for each statement in the code coverage intersection is created, its edges are generated, and recurse. For example, considering the sequence coverage in Fig. 4, the algorithm starts by defining the least instance for a: (1, 2, 1), and the least instance for b: (2, 3, 2) and adds them to a stack. Then, it picks (1, 2, 1) from the stack, generates its edges by choosing from the *next least possible* instances relative to it, and adds those next least possible instances back to the stack if they do not already exist or if they have not been already processed. To generate the next least possible instances efficiently, binary search is used by constructing an array $pos[s, t_i]$ storing the positions of each statement s in each sequence cover of t_i in sorted order. Given an instance $(p_1, \ldots, p_m)$ of a statement s', the next least position to p_i is found in the sequence of t_i by searching for p_i in that sequence. Consuming nodes from the stack are continued until the stack becomes empty, the point at which a precedence graph is generated on the instances, where any path in that graph represents a common subsequence between the execution traces of all test cases.

Definition 9. (Common subsequences graph) A common subsequences graph is a directed acyclic graph whose nodes represent instances of occurrence of statements in the sequence cover of all test cases, and its edges represent the direct $<$ relationship between those instances. Any path in this graph represents a common subsequence of the execution traces of all test cases.

4.3.3 Extracting Common Subsequences

To generate the common subsequences between the execution traces of all test cases, the algorithm starts from the node representing the failure statement in the common subsequences graph, and traverses its neighbors, generates all possible paths. Each of these paths is a common subsequence. Algorithm 1 lists the pseudocode for the common subsequence extraction process.

ALGORITHM 1 Common Subsequences Generation Algorithm

```
 1: procedure GET_COMMON_SUBSEQUENCE
 2:    C = C(t₁) ∩ C(t₂) ∩ ...C(tₙ)
 3:    for statement s ∈ C do
 4:        for test case ∈ tᵢ do
 5:            pos[s, tᵢ] = all the positions of stmt s ∈ S(tᵢ)
 6:        end for
 7:    end for
 8:    for statement s ∈ C do
 9:        for test case ∈ tᵢ do
10:            min_instance[s, i] = − 1
11:        end for
12:    end for
13:    for statement s ∈ C do
14:        for test case ∈ tᵢ do
15:            min_instance[s, i] =
16:            min(pos[s, tᵢ]) s.t. pos[s, tᵢ] >
17:            min_instance[s, i]
18:        end for
19:        instances = instances ∪ min_instance[s]
20:    end for
21:    while instances is not empty do
22:        inst = pop(instances)
23:        for statement s ∈ C do
24:            instᶜ = least instance i of s such that i > inst
25:            if instᶜ ! = null then
26:                pred[instᶜ] = pred[instᶜ] ∪ inst
27:                if instᶜ does not exist in instances && instᶜ was not processed
           before then
28:                    instances = instances ∪ instᶜ
29:                end if
30:            end if
31:        end for
32:    end while
33:    starting from the failure statements in the graph, generate all
       possible paths
34: end procedure
```

4.3.4 Algorithm Optimizations

The developed algorithm is enhanced by (1) abstracting the test cases, and (2) extracting the most important subsequences only. Test case abstractions transform the sequence covers to more abstract, shorter versions. Most important subsequence extraction selects a subsequence from the common subsequences graph that is most likely to contain the faulty line.

4.3.5 Test Case Abstraction

Test case abstraction is achieved using two techniques: loop-based abstraction and block-based abstraction.

4.3.5.1 Loop-Based Abstraction

While creating the graph of instances, it is found that the algorithm spent a lot of time and memory in building the graph because of the existence of repeated lines resulting from program loops. Loops result in lines that are repeated multiple times in each sequence cover, and their occurrence in multiple sequence covers results in a number of instances in the graph that is exponentially proportional to the number of test cases. Therefore, this approach is impractical. Furthermore, from the developer's point of view, inspecting a single occurrence of each line in the loop may be more convenient than inspecting all iterations of the loop unrolled. Therefore, before extracting the intersected lines among all the test cases, each loop in each test case sequence is compressed to appear as one iteration. Loops are identified as any subsequence of program lines in the execution trace that is consecutively repeated more than once. Note that this does not affect the variable values reported to the developer as part of the tool output, as those values are extracted anyway for each iteration of the loop as part of the variable value extraction technique discussed in Section 4.3.8. Therefore, although the line appears once in the results, all possible variable values are still preserved.

4.3.5.2 Block-Based Abstraction

Furthermore, another observation is that there are program lines in the sequence cover of each test case which always appear consecutively either within the same test case or across all the test cases. So, there is no need to build graph instances for each line individually while one instance can be created for all of them together representing a single block, and hence, save a lot of time and memory. Therefore, an efficient technique is developed for identifying consecutive lines of code that are shared between all the test cases. After extracting these common consecutive lines and representing them as individual blocks in the instance graph, those blocks are mapped back to their corresponding lines while outputting the results to the developer.

The approach for extracting common consecutive subsequences among all test cases is nontrivial. The first approach is constructing the graph containing all instances, and extracting paths whose instances are before each other by *exactly one position*, which guarantees that the resulting subsequences are consecutive in each test case. However, this approach does not work for tests with large sequences as building the graph is still very time consuming, which defeats the purpose of efficiently building and processing the graph. On the other hand, the graph with a subset of the instances that are only consecutive to each other could not be built, as this still requires to consider all possible graph instances in order to find out whether they have consecutive neighbors or not.

In order to extract consecutive common subsequences efficiently, the developed approach starts from common subsequences within each test case separately, which significantly reduces the search space. For each test case, the suffix tree algorithm is used to extract all repeated consecutive subsequences in that test case, where the entire test case sequence is treated as a string, and each line in that sequence as a character in the suffix tree string. The output of that process is a set of subsequences which are repeated multiple times within the test case. Note that those subsequences vary in their length and number of repetitions, which affects their abstraction power, where subsequences with higher length and number of repetitions have more abstraction power over those with less. Those subsequences may also overlap, where applying one of them (i.e., using it to compress the test case into individual blocks) may invalidate the possibility of applying others. Therefore, to address these two issues, each subsequence is assigned a score, that is, the result of multiplying its length by its number of repetitions, and hence, each subsequence is associated with a measure of its importance or abstraction power. This consecutive repeated subsequence detection process is applied for each sequence cover, and after extracting the repeated consecutive subsequences for each test case, the set of those repeated subsequences are intersected across all sequence covers to identify the blocks that appear in *all* sequences multiple times. The score of each subsequence in the intersection is updated to be the sum of its scores in the individual sequences to reflect its abstraction power relative to all sequences. Finally, the subsequences are sorted according to their scores and apply them in order. Note that we cannot substitute subsequences locally in each test case sequence without ensuring that the subsequence exists in other test case sequences as well, as this will hide lines underlying each block, which can be shared across all sequences, but cannot be seen when represented as a single block that does not necessarily appear in all test cases. Therefore, by making sure the blocks appear in all sequences, we know that the underlying lines match among those blocks in all sequences as well, and hence, are still be seen in the final output.

One final optimization is related to the suffix tree construction algorithm, which may not scale to very large test case sequences with tens of thousands of lines of code. The test case sequence is partitioned to a number of partitions, each with a smaller number of lines in the sequence, apply the suffix tree algorithm to each partition, and finally union the resulting subsequences from each partition and update their scores accordingly.

4.3.6 Extracting the Most Important Subsequences

Traversing all the paths starting from the throwing exception node in large graphs is time consuming, results in a large number of paths, and may cause out of memory exceptions, while we are only interested in just one sequence to present to the user, which should highly likely contain the trace back from the throwing line to the source line. Therefore, in the developed algorithm, instead of traversing all paths, scores are assigned to the nodes in the graph according to their degrees, which indicate the likelihood of those nodes participating in faulty sequences, and then the path that passes along the nodes with the highest scores is generated.

4.3.7 Hybrid Dynamic/Static Analysis

Although the number of the statements in the output common subsequence can be small after applying the abstraction techniques discussed above, they can still include some statements that do not have any effect on failing statement. These statements may be a source of distraction to the developer while backtracking the common subsequence to find the source of the error.

To backtrack the lines, call and data dependency information of the program are employed. Obtaining the common subsequences between the execution traces has an advantage. The existence of those common subsequences enables us to avoid expanding the entire dependency graph of the entire program. Therefore, in order to extract these dependencies efficiently, the common subsequences is utilized to restrict the search space of the dependency graph. This is done by generating the call graph for only the subset of the classes and the methods that appear in the common statement subsequence. For each method, the def/use graph is built of their statements. This graph contains a node for each statement, and there is an edge between two nodes if a control can flow from one node to the other one. At the same time, the dependency of the failure statement is extracted and the dependency is restricted to the subset of statements appearing in the common subsequence. There are three main algorithms that are used to achieve this type of hybrid dynamic/static analysis:

1. In the first algorithm, the call graph of the methods that the statements of the common subsequence belong to is generated. This procedure is stated in Algorithm 2.

ALGORITHM 2 Call Graph Generation Algorithm

```
1: procedure GET_CALL_GRAPH(Sequence q)
2:     for statement s ∈ q do
3:         classes = classes ∪ s.class_name
4:     end for
5:     g = Generate_Call_Graph(classes)
6:     return g
7: end procedure
```

2. To get the def/use *chain* of an individual statement, the variables and the methods that are referenced in that statement are extracted. Then, for the referenced variables, the statements that assign these variables are added to the *chain*. The variables could be passed as method parameters, in which case the assigning statement is found in the calling method which passes the parameter value, and hence step 1 is used to obtain the calling-callee information. For the referenced methods, their return statements are added(if any) to the chain, in addition to any statements that change nonlocal variables. This procedure is listed in Algorithm 3.

ALGORITHM 3 Def/Use Chain Extraction Algorithm

```
1: procedure GET_DEFUSE_CHAIN(Statement s, Sequence q)
2:     g = Get_Call_Graph(q)
3:     uses = get_referenced_methods_and_vars(s)
4:     for e ∈ uses do                          ▷ e could be a variable or method
5:         if e is a variable then
6:             if e is passed as the enclosing method m parameter then
7:                 m' = g.get_calling(m)
8:                 e' = variable corresponding to e in m'
9:                 s' = get_assigning_stmt(e', m')
10:            else
11:                s' = get_assigning_stmt(e, m)
12:            end if
13:            chain = chain ∪ s'
14:        else                                  ▷ e is a method
15:            chain = chain ∪ return_stmts(e)
16:            chain = chain ∪
17:                stmts_assigning_non_local_vars(e)
18:        end if
19:    end for
20:    return chain
21: end procedure
```

3. Now, starting from the failure statement, its dependencies are got as outlined in the previous step and for each dependency (element of the *chain*), the algorithm recurses on it *only if* it is part of the common subsequence obtained in Section 4.3.4. This procedure is listed in Algorithm 4. The inputs for that procedure are the call graph, the failure statement, the *in* sequence, which is initialized to the common subsequence generated as discussed in Section 4.3.4, and the *out* sequence, which is initialized to ϕ for the first call.

To implement this hybrid analysis, Soot [73] is used. Soot is a software engineering tool for analyzing and optimizing Java programs. It provides program call graph and intraprocedural data flow analysis. For the intraprocedural data flow analysis, it operates on a control-flow graph called UnitGraph.

4.3.8 Remote Debugging

This step is responsible of extracting the variable values. It takes the common subsequence and the application source code as inputs and outputs each line

ALGORITHM 4 Dependency Extraction Algorithm

```
 1: procedure GET_DEPENDENCIES(Stmt s, Call_Graph g, Sequence in, Sequence out)
 2:     out' = out ∪ s
 3:     chain = Get_DefUse_Chain(s)
 4:     for s' ∈ chain do
 5:         if s' ∈ in then
 6:             Get_Dependencies(s, g, in, out')
 7:         end if
 8:     end for
 9:     return out'
10: end procedure
```

attached with each variable values. Since in this research Java applications are used, the Java Debugger (JDB) [74] command line debugging tool is used to automate extracting the variable values. JDB is a full-fledged Java debugging tool that is based on Java Platform Debugger Architecture that provides inspection and debugging of a local or remote Java virtual machines. It allows setting breakpoints, stepping, and suspending on exceptions, all through a command line interface. A script that automatically sets debugging breakpoints at the lines of the program constituting the common subsequence, steps over those breakpoints, and dumps the values of the variables appearing in those lines is written. Variable values in a line can only be retrieved after the line has been fully executed, including any methods that it may call. If those methods have breakpoints too, which is usually the case, we keep track of the method call stack, in order to remember a line when we return back to its method after its execution, as JDB does not simply return to the same line after it exhausts the entire call stack, and at the same time, does not necessarily return to the line next to it in cases like if statements or loops. Therefore, there is no built-in way in this case to know at which point variables values can be already extracted so that they express the state of the program directly after executing a particular line, and hence, a new approach is implemented on top of JDB.

5. CONCLUSION

In this chapter, *Disqover*, a new fault localization technique, was presented. This technique exploits automated test case generation tools to generate a large number of test cases and implements a novel algorithm to find commonalities between the failing test cases by automatically replaying them, and extracting their sequence covers, i.e., execution traces. As debugging costs continue to be more expensive, the benefits of automated debugging and fault localization techniques will become more tangible. Nowadays, static analysis methods are so advanced and integrated in pretty much all of software development IDEs. Also, software instrumentation techniques are prevalent, and it is not uncommon to have instrumented versions of software in a production setting for various dynamic analysis purposes. However, either technique, static or dynamic, is not sufficient by itself to accurately identify software faults. Hybrid approaches can make static and dynamic approaches complement each other to achieve the best of the two worlds. In this chapter, we presented one such approach, and we hope it attracts the research community attention to the value of hybrid approaches. Such approaches are not limited to improve fault localization only, but also performance testing, memory profiling, and software structure and quality in general.

REFERENCES

[1] I. Vessey, Expertise in debugging computer programs: a process analysis, Int. J. Man Mach. Stud. 23 (5) (1985) 459–494.

[2] G.J. Myers, The Art of Software Testing, second ed., Wiley, New York, 2004, ISBN 978-0-471-46912-4, I–XV, 234 pp.

[3] P. Godefroid, J. de Halleux, A.V. Nori, S.K. Rajamani, W. Schulte, N. Tillmann, M.Y. Levin, Automating software testing using program analysis, IEEE Softw. 25 (5) (2008) 30–37.

[4] Q. Xie, A.M. Memon, Using a pilot study to derive a GUI model for automated testing, ACM Trans. Softw. Eng. Methodol. 18 (2) (2008).

[5] A.M. Memon, Q. Xie, Studying the fault-detection effectiveness of GUI test cases for rapidly evolving software, IEEE Trans. Softw. Eng. 31 (10) (2005) 884–896, ISSN 0098-5589.

[6] F. Belli, Finite-state testing and analysis of graphical user interfaces, in: ISSRE, 2001, pp. 34–43.

[7] F. Belli, C.J. Budnik, L. White, Event-based modelling, analysis and testing of user interactions: approach and case study, Softw. Test. Verif. Reliab. 16 (1) (2006) 3–32.

[8] A.C.R. Paiva, N. Tillmann, J.C.P. Faria, R.F.A.M. Vidal, Modeling and testing hierarchical GUIs, in: Abstract State Machines, 2005, pp. 329–344.

[9] R.K. Shehady, D.P. Siewiorek, A method to automate user interface testing using variable finite state machines, in: Proceedings of the 27th International Symposium on Fault-Tolerant Computing (FTCS '97), IEEE Computer Society, Washington, DC, USA, ISBN 0-8186-7831-3, 1997, p. 80.

[10] L. Wang, J. Yuan, X. Yu, J. Hu, X. Li, G. Zheng, Generating test cases from UML activity diagram based on Gray-Box method, in: APSEC, 2004, pp. 284–291.

[11] H. Kim, S. Kang, J. Baik, I.-Y. Ko, Test cases generation from UML activity diagrams, in: SNPD, vol. 3, 2007, pp. 556–561.

[12] M. Chen, P. Mishra, D. Kalita, Coverage-driven automatic test generation for UML activity diagrams, in: ACM Great Lakes Symposium on VLSI, 2008, pp. 139–142.

[13] M. Chen, X. Qiu, X. Li, Automatic test case generation for UML activity diagrams, in: AST, 2006, pp. 2–8.

[14] M. Chen, X. Qiu, W. Xu, L. Wang, J. Zhao, X. Li, UML Activity diagram-based automatic test case generation for Java programs, Comput. J. 52 (5) (2009) 545–556.

[15] C.-Y. Huang, J.-H. Lo, S.-Y. Kuo, M.R. Lyu, Software reliability modeling and cost estimation incorporating testing-effort and efficiency, in: Proceedings of the 10th International Symposium on Software Reliability Engineering (ISSRE'99), 1999, pp. 62–72.

[16] T. Dinh-Trong, A systematic approach to testing UML design models, in: Doctorial Symposium, 7th International Conference on the Unified Modeling Language, Lisbon, Portugal, 2004.

[17] P. Samuel, A.T. Joseph, Test sequence generation from UML sequence diagrams, in: SNPD, 2008, pp. 879–887.

[18] M. Sarma, D. Kundu, R. Mall, Automatic test case generation from UML sequence diagrams, in: Proceedings of the 15th International Conference on Advanced Computing and Communications, IEEE Computer Society, 2007, pp. 60–67.

[19] A.Z. Javed, P.A. Strooper, G. Watson, Automated generation of test cases using model-driven architecture, in: AST, 2007, pp. 3–9.

[20] N. Ismail, R. Ibrahim, N. Ibrahim, Automatic generation of test cases from use-case diagram, in: Proceedings of the International Conference on Electrical Engineering and Informatics Institut Teknologi, Bandung, Indonesia, 2007.

[21] S.K. Swain, D.P. Mohapatra, Article:test case generation from behavioral UML Models, Int. J. Comput. Appl. 6 (8) (2010) 5–11 (published By Foundation of Computer Science).

[22] M. Riebisch, I. Philippow, M. Götze, UML-based statistical test case generation, in: NetObjectDays, 2002, pp. 394–411.

[23] S. Ali, L.C. Briand, M.J.-U. Rehman, H. Asghar, M.Z.Z. Iqbal, A. Nadeem, A state-based approach to integration testing based on UML models, Inform. Softw. Technol. 49 (11–12) (2007) 1087–1106.

[24] S. Ogata, S. Matsuura, Towards the reliable integration testing: UML-based scenario analysis using an automatic prototype generation tool, in: Proceedings of the 9th WSEAS International Conference on Software Engineering, Parallel and Distributed Systems, SEPADS'10, World Scientific and Engineering Academy and Society (WSEAS), Stevens Point, Wisconsin, USA, ISBN 978-960-474-156-4, 2010, pp. 151–159. http://dl.acm.org/citation.cfm?id=1807733.1807758.

[25] S. Ogata, S. Matsuura, S. Ogata, S. Matsuura, A method of automatic integration test case generation from UML-based Scenario, WSEAS Trans. Inform. Sci. Appl. 7 (2010) 598–607.

[26] C. Pfaller, Requirements-based test case specification by using information from model construction, in: AST, 2008, pp. 7–16.

[27] A. Cavarra, C. Crichton, J. Davies, A. Hartman, L. Mounier, Using UML for automatic test generation, in: International Symposium on Software Testing and Analysis ISSTA, Springer-Verlag, Berlin, 2002.

[28] Q. Farooq, M.Z.Z. Iqbal, Z.I. Malik, A. Nadeem, An approach for selective state machine based regression testing, in: A-MOST, 2007, pp. 44–52.

[29] V. Garousi, L.C. Briand, Y. Labiche, Control flow analysis of UML 2.0 sequence diagrams, in: Model Driven Architecture—Foundations and Applications, ECMDA-FA, Springer, Berlin, Heidelberg, 2005, pp. 160–174.

[30] A. Alhroob, K.P. Dahal, M.A. Hossain, Automatic test cases generation from software specifications, e-Informatica 4 (1) (2010) 109–121.

[31] A.M. Memon, An event-flow model of GUI-based applications for testing, Softw. Test. Verif. Rel. 17 (3) (2007) 137–157, ISSN 0960-0833.

[32] X. Yuan, A.M. Memon, Generating event sequence-based test cases using GUI runtime state feedback. IEEE Trans. Softw. Eng. 36 (1) (2010) 81–95, ISSN 0098-5589, http://dx.doi.org/10.1109/TSE.2009.68.

[33] G. Perrouin, S. Sen, J. Klein, B. Baudry, Y.L. Traon, Automated and scalable T-wise test case generation strategies for software product lines, in: ICST, IEEE Computer Society, Washington, DC, USA, 2010, pp. 459–468.

[34] S. Gnesi, D. Latella, M. Massink, Formal test-case generation for UML statecharts, in: Proc. 9th IEEE Int. Conf. on Engineering of Complex Computer Systems, IEEE Computer Society, 2004, pp. 75–84.

[35] M. Weiser, Program slicing, IEEE Trans. Software Eng. 10 (4) (1984) 352–357.

[36] M. Weiser, Programmers use slices when debugging, Commun. ACM 25 (7) (1982) 446–452.

[37] H. Agrawal, J.R. Horgan, Dynamic program slicing, in: PLDI, 1990, pp. 246–256.

[38] R.A. DeMillo, H. Pan, E.H. Spafford, Critical slicing for software fault localization, in: ISSTA, 1996, pp. 121–134.

[39] T. Gyimothy, A. Beszedes, I. Forgacs, An efficient relevant slicing method for debugging, in: ESEC/SIGSOFT FSE, 1999, pp. 303–321.

[40] X. Zhang, N. Gupta, R. Gupta, Pruning dynamic slices with confidence, in: PLDI, 2006, pp. 169–180.

[41] X. Zhang, R. Gupta, Y. Zhang, Precise dynamic slicing algorithms, in: ICSE, 2003, pp. 319–329.

[42] B. Ness, V. Ngo, Regression containment through source change isolation, in: COMPSAC '97: Proceedings of the 21st International Computer Software and Applications Conference, IEEE Computer Society, Washington, DC, USA, ISBN 0-8186-8105-5, 1997, pp. 616–621.

[43] T.W. Reps, T. Ball, M. Das, J.R. Larus, The use of program profiling for software maintenance with applications to the year 2000 problem, in: ESEC/SIGSOFT FSE, Springer, Berlin, Heidelberg, 1997, pp. 432–449.

[44] T. Ball, M. Naik, S.K. Rajamani, From symptom to cause: localizing errors in counterexample traces, in: POPL, 2003, pp. 97–105.

[45] A. Groce, D. Kroening, F. Lerda, Understanding counterexamples with explain, in: CAV, Springer, Berlin, Heidelberg, 2004, pp. 453–456.

[46] L. Naish, H.J. Lee, K. Ramamohanarao, A model for spectra-based software diagnosis. ACM Trans. Softw. Eng. Methodol. 20 (3) (2011) 11, http://dx.doi.org/10.1145/2000791.2000795.

[47] J.A. Jones, M.J. Harrold, J.T. Stasko, Visualization of test information to assist fault localization, in: ICSE, 2002, pp. 467–477.

[48] S. Moon, Y. Kim, M. Kim, S. Yoo, Ask the mutants: mutating faulty programs for fault localization. in: Seventh IEEE International Conference on Software Testing, Verification and Validation, ICST 2014, March 31 2014–April 4, 2014, Cleveland, Ohio, USA, 2014, pp. 153–162, http://dx.doi.org/10.1109/ICST.2014.28.

[49] B. Liblit, M. Naik, A.X. Zheng, A. Aiken, M.I. Jordan, Scalable statistical bug isolation, in: PLDI, 2005, pp. 15–26.

[50] C. Liu, X. Yan, L. Fei, J. Han, S.P. Midkiff, SOBER: statistical model-based bug localization, in: ESEC/SIGSOFT FSE, 2005, pp. 286–295.

[51] A. Zeller, Isolating cause-effect chains from computer programs, in: SIGSOFT FSE, 2002, pp. 1–10.

[52] H. Cleve, A. Zeller, Locating causes of program failures, in: ICSE, 2005, pp. 342–351.

[53] J. Ruthruff, E.R. Creswick, M. Burnett, C. Cook, S. Prabhakararao, M.F. Ii, M. Main, End-user software visualizations for fault localization. in: SoftVis '03: Proceedings of the 2003 ACM symposium on Software visualization, ACM Press, San Diego, CA, USA, ISBN 1581136420, 2003, pp. 123–132, http://dx.doi.org/10.1145/774833.774851.

[54] E. Wong, T. Wei, Y. Qi, L. Zhao, A crosstab-based statistical method for effective fault localization. in: Proceedings of the 2008 International Conference on Software Testing, Verification, and Validation, IEEE Computer Society, Washington, DC, USA, ISBN 978-0-7695-3127-4, 2008, pp. 42–51, http://dx.doi.org/10.1109/ICST.2008.65.

[55] Z. Zhang, W.K. Chan, T.H. Tse, Fault localization based only on failed runs, IEEE Comput. 45 (6) (2012) 64–71, http://dx.doi.org/10.1109/MC.2012.185.

[56] W.E. Wong, Y. Qi, Bp neural network-based effective fault localization, Int. J. Softw. Eng. Know. 19 (4) (2009) 573–597.

[57] W.E. Wong, Y. Shi, Y. Qi, R. Golden, Using an RBF neural network to locate program bugs, in: ISSRE, 2008, pp. 27–36.

[58] L.C. Briand, Y. Labiche, X. Liu, Using machine learning to support debugging with tarantula, in: ISSRE, 2007, pp. 137–146.

[59] Y. Brun, M.D. Ernst, Finding latent code errors via machine learning over program executions, in: ICSE, 2004, pp. 480–490.

[60] S. Nessa, M. Abedin, W.E. Wong, L. Khan, Y. Qi, Software fault localization using N-gram analysis, in: WASA, Springer, Berlin, Heidelberg, 2008, pp. 548–559.

[61] P. Cellier, M. Ducassé, S. Ferré, O. Ridoux, Formal concept analysis enhances fault localization in software, in: ICFCA, 2008, pp. 273–288.

[62] F. Wotawa, M. Stumptner, W. Mayer, Model-based debugging or how to diagnose programs automatically, in: IEA/AIE, 2002, pp. 746–757.

[63] C. Mateis, M. Stumptner, F. Wotawa, Modeling Java programs for diagnosis, in: Proceedings of the European Conference on Artificial Intelligence (ECAI 2000), 2000.

[64] W. Mayer, M. Stumptner, Modeling programs with unstructured control flow for debugging, in: Australian Joint Conference on Artificial Intelligence, 2002, pp. 107–118.

[65] W. Mayer, M. Stumptner, F. Wotawa, Debugging program exceptions, in: Proc. DX'03 Workshop, 2003, pp. 119–124.

[66] R.A. DeMillo, H. Pan, E.H. Spafford, Failure and fault analysis for software debugging, in: COMPSAC, 1997, pp. 515–521.

[67] G. Ammons, J. Choi, M. Gupta, N. Swamy, Finding and removing performance bottlenecks in large systems, in: Proceedings of ECOOP, Springer, Berlin, 2004.

[68] K. Srinivas, H. Srinivasan, Summarizing application performance from a components perspective, in: Proceedings of the 10th European Software Engineering Conference Held Jointly with 13th ACM SIGSOFT International Symposium on Foundations of Software Engineering, ACM, New York, NY, USA, ISBN 1-59593-014-0, 2005, pp. 136–145, http://dx.doi.org/10.1145/1081706.1081730.

[69] G. Sevitsky, W.D. Pauw, R. Konuru, An information exploration tool for performance analysis of Java programs, in: TOOLS (38), IEEE Computer Society, ISBN 0-7695-1095-7, 2001, pp. 85–101. http://dblp.uni-trier.de/db/conf/tools/tools38-2001.html#SevitskyPK01.

[70] S. Han, Y. Dang, S. Ge, D. Zhang, T. Xie, Performance debugging in the large via mining millions of stack traces, in: ICSE, 2012, pp. 145–155.

[71] E.R. Altman, M. Arnold, S. Fink, N. Mitchell, Performance analysis of idle programs, in: OOPSLA, 2010, pp. 739–753.

[72] Cobertura (A code coverage utility for Java), n.d., http://cobertura.github.io/cobertura/.

[73] R. Vallée-Rai, P. Co, E. Gagnon, L.J. Hendren, P. Lam, V. Sundaresan, Soot—a Java bytecode optimization framework, in: Proceedings of the 1999 Conference of the Centre for Advanced Studies on Collaborative Research, November 8–11, 1999, Mississauga, Ontario, Canada, 1999, p. 13.

[74] jdb - The Java Debugger, n.d., http://docs.oracle.com/javase/7/docs/technotes/tools/windows/jdb.html.

ABOUT THE AUTHOR

Ethar Elsaka is a PhD graduate from the University of Maryland. Her research interests are in automated software debugging and improving developer productivity. She has a number of publications on GUI testing, hybrid static and dynamic analysis of software for fault localization, and how to build practical tools that can leverage these approaches, and make them usable by software developers.

CHAPTER FOUR

Characterizing Software Test Case Behavior With Regression Models

B. Robbins
Siemens PLM Software, Huntsville, AL, United States

Contents

Advances in Computers, Volume 105
ISSN 0065-2458
http://dx.doi.org/10.1016/bs.adcom.2016.12.002

115

Abstract

Testing modern software applications, such as those built on an event-driven paradigm, requires effective consideration of context. Model-based testing (MBT) approaches have been presented as an effective way to consider context, but effective MBT requires a high level of automation. Fully automated approaches too often lead to issues that threaten the very claims that MBT offers, such as generating test cases which are not fully executable and generating very large suites of test cases. In this chapter, I describe a new class of models for automated MBT workflows: predictive regression models. I compare these models with those in a state-of-the-art automated MBT workflow. I also describe a modern infrastructure to execute large MBT suites, to counter the seed suite required to construct predictive regression models, and to further enable effective MBT approaches in general. I conclude with a summary of recent research that effectively applied a regression model for test case feasibility as a filter for automatically generated test cases.

As a discipline, automated, model-based testing (MBT) of software has been around for decades. However, MBT approaches have largely struggled to cross over into practical industry applications. Fully automated approaches to MBT of modern applications have shown promise, but still suffer from a number of issues.

In this chapter, I show that a class of predictive regression models developed from a feedback loop can be used to enhance existing MBT approaches. The techniques I present here within the context of model-based graphical user interface (GUI) software are also applicable to the even broader category of "event-driven software" (EDS).

In Section 1, I frame and motivate traditional challenges in testing GUI software and present a set of problems presented by current MBT approaches. In Section 2, I provide additional background, both in MBT approaches and in predictive regression models. In Section 3, I present an updated MBT workflow enabled by state-of-the-art tools for automated MBT and the consideration of predictive regression models. In Section 4, I describe a scalable framework for large-scale execution of MBT test cases, which supports the scale of MBT and regression model construction. I conclude in Section 5 with a summary of recent research applying regression models to the *feasibility problem* from MBT.

The content of this chapter is adapted from my recent dissertation on the same topic [1], which may be referred to for additional reading on the subject. A number of figures and tables in this chapter have been reused from that publication with permission.

1. MOTIVATION

1.1 Finding Bugs in Software

Software "bugs" are notoriously difficult to find. Even companies spending billions on their software still find themselves humbled by problems after release. Some now argue that writing bug-free software is practically impossible (or at best, not cost effective). The high-stakes economy around technology also presents its own trade-offs, as the cost of being late to market is often much higher than the cost of fixing bugs.

But what do we even mean by the colloquial term *bug*? At a high level, the real problem is that the software did not behave as expected. In practice, there are many people who have expectations about the behavior of any given software application: the end-users, the owners, the maintainers, and so on. Before we go on, we need a much more general (yet more precise) definition.

IEEE Standard 1044 [2] provides a definition for a "defect" as "an imperfection or deficiency in a work product where that work product does not meet its requirements or specifications." Importantly, defects can occur throughout the Software Development Life Cycle (SDLC). The artifacts of so-called *early-life cycle phases* of the SDLC, such as requirements gathering and design, can have defects. Defects in these artifacts can carry through to downstream artifacts such as source code and binaries. Defects which occur in the running executable components of a software application are often classified as failures (departures from the expected behavior of the application) or faults (any manifestation of a human error in a piece of software).

For the purposes of this chapter, I will not typically distinguish between the different types of defects in software applications. I do, however, assert that the *quality* of artifacts is a function of the defects present. Furthermore, I assert that every defect detected and removed from a piece of software improves the quality of that software. While there are many trade-offs to consider, finding and fixing defects as quickly as possible remains an important goal in modern-day software development.

1.2 Software Quality Assurance Activities

Within the SDLC, there are a number of Quality Assurance (QA) activities focused on measuring and assuring the quality of software. Whether or not these activities are done by a separate group of people, or during a separate phase of development, the same questions are addressed:

- *Planning*: How should each artifact be checked for defects?
- *Finding potential defects*: Given the requirements or expectations of an artifact, are there any potential "imperfections or deficiencies" present?
- *Triaging potential defects*: Does each potential defect really qualify as a defect? If so, what is the likelihood and impact of the defect?

While there are certainly interesting considerations and techniques for Planning and Triaging, the act of finding potential defects continues to receive the most attention in industry and research. There are many categories of defect-finding approaches applicable for executable software artifacts, such as:

- *Compilation or interpretation*: Source code translates into executable formats, and this process requires parsing and semantic analysis that may reveal defects related to conformance to the programming language.
- *Static analysis*: Tools can inspect source code or compiled code for common mistakes.
- *Reviews*: Team members can read one another's source code and offer feedback on possible defects.
- *Testing*: Executable artifacts can be evaluated by running and inspecting their output under certain conditions.

While the other techniques listed above are certainly valuable [3, 4], *software testing* continues to be the most ubiquitous defect-finding technique in software development. Entire development methodologies in the industry (such as the very popular test-driven development technique [5]) have been developed around the idea of testing early and often. Perhaps some of this is due to the "pass/fail" nature of tests—their status, as opposed to review feedback, is nonnegotiable. At the system level, executable tests are also at the user level, which helps to build confidence that lower-level approaches cannot provide.

1.3 Software Testing Activities

Within software testing as a discipline, a great deal of work related to testing a piece of software actually occurs prior to test execution.

In *test suite design*, testers develop requirements for a collection of tests, referred to as *coverage criteria*. In the industry, I have seen test suites developed around coverage of all requirements, all user interface (UI) components, all new features for a release, all web server endpoints, and other like-minded criteria. The same application often requires multiple test suites, each with a targeted goal that may also be mapped to the application's own delivery life cycle. Efficiency is often a driver for test suite design as well. In an ideal world, we would simply run every test against every code check in; but this would only be feasible for the most trivial application or suite of tests.

Once a tester designs a test suite, he or she will *construct test cases* to be added to suites. The test cases for a specific suite should collectively achieve the coverage criteria of the test suite. If I aim, for example, to cover all UI components in my application, I may first collect a list of all UI components and then craft a special test case for each component, to ensure that every component is covered.

Test cases take the form $\langle I, E \rangle$, where I describes some input to the application, and E represents any expected output to be verified against actual output during test case execution. These sets can both include multiple elements: a test case can require any number of inputs, and require asserting that any number of outputs match expectations. Constructing a test case, then, involves selecting a set of inputs (and potentially, their order or other relationships between them) and a set of expected outputs to be verified.

In addition, testers must also *maintain test cases and test suites* across multiple application development cycles or releases. For example, a test suite with a goal of covering all requirements of an application must be updated any time a requirement is added, removed, or changed. Understandably, this may require creating new test cases or repairing old ones.

Repair may also be necessary any time an interface is used by the test changes. Many testing strategies in industry are designed to execute against interfaces that are less likely to change, or interfaces that require less effort to change. For example, tests that execute against an application programming interface (API) layer instead of a UI layer often run much quicker and require less maintenance to update.

At a higher level, testers can *develop an overall testing strategy* which drives the design of test suites, creation of test cases, and maintenance of these artifacts. This higher-level view is critical for optimization and proper management of testing activities. For example, many test cases will be appropriate for more than one test suite and should not be maintained separately in isolation. Even within a single test suite, individual test cases designed with targeted goals tend to overlap, wasting resources, and maintenance effort. An effective strategy balances the important variables of testing effort and defect risk.

For example, the decision to define application tests at the API level instead of the UI level has trade-offs in terms of risks. As I discuss in much more detail below, the UI level often introduces its own bugs (i.e., that could not be discovered by API tests at all) and often exercises bugs that are not obvious from consideration of API layers alone.

1.4 Testing EDS

The activities outlined above may seem complex enough already, but so far, we have only considered a very simplified case. Today's most popular software applications, including those on Web, mobile, and Desktop platforms, are almost always built on event processing. Users (or often, other system actors) perform events. These events produce output and may also affect application state. This event-driven paradigm presents several challenges for the software testing activities introduced above.

We can think of a simple event-driven application as shown in Fig. 1. The application defines an interface, and an actor somehow submits events to this interface. Once the system receives the event, it may or may not immediately respond and may or may not update its own state. Typically, the actor can proceed to carry out additional events against the

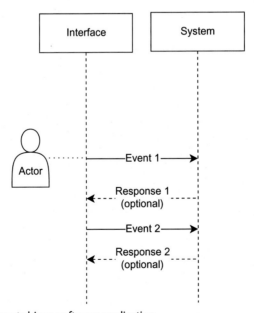

Fig. 1 A basic event-driven software application.

system which may or may not be related to (or have any effect on) any previous events.

While we would like to think of the event-driven paradigm as a simplification for testing thanks to its isolation of user actions to targeted bits of event-handling code, the so-called side effects that change application state and potentially impact subsequent events make testing event-driven software a challenge.

The ability of actors to perform events in sequence blurs the boundary between traditional notions of input and output in software testing. The outputs of one event become the input of the next. The input to each test case can itself be a sequence of events designed to set up application state for any necessary verifications. The verifications themselves can be applied at any point in the input sequence. Fig. 2 contrasts event-driven test cases with their predecessors.

Under this new model, it is clear that effective testing of event-driven software requires consideration of the software and any integrated systems' context throughout all testing activities. By *context*, I mean the *state* of a running software component or integrated system. When carrying out QA activities on event-driven software, we must consider the effects of this state.

Table 1 details a number of potential considerations of event context throughout the SDLC.

Traditionally, every necessary input event or verification added to a test case stands to increase the number of possible test cases required for effective testing exponentially. Considerations of context have analogous exponential effects on the testing of event-driven software.

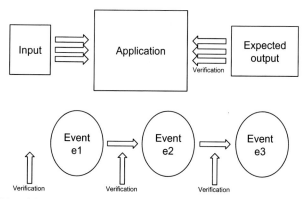

Fig. 2 Traditional (*top*) vs event-based test cases (*bottom*).

Table 1 Considerations of Context in Testing of Event-Driven Applications

Testing Activity	Considerations of Context
Test suite design	Sequence-based coverage criteria on various event domains Sampling according to event sequence characteristics
Test case construction	Control and evaluate contribution to sequence-based coverage criteria
Test case execution	Collect runtime event execution feedback on various event domains
Test suite maintenance	Minimize duplicate sequence coverage Compare sequence coverage between test suites
Test case maintenance	Evaluate contribution to coverage criteria

In the example event-based test case from Fig. 2, the verification performed after $e2$ must take into account not only the effects of $e2$ but also any residual effects of $e1$ and the interaction between $e1$ and $e2$. The verification may even need to compensate for the existing state of an application prior to the execution of the current test case, for example, if the application is in any way sensitive to previously entered data. Often, testers can control for intertest dependencies by applying techniques such as "testing the delta" (i.e., designing the test and its verifications to ignore unrelated data). Clearly, testers must *consider the context* of event execution when constructing test cases for event-driven systems.

The same effects appear in other QA activities as well. Testers must also consider context during test suite design. Verifying the correct functionality of $e2$ after the execution of the sequence $e1$ does not directly imply correct functionality of $e2$ after the execution of any other sequence. Therefore, a test suite designed to verify the correct functionality of $e2$ may have to consider the execution of $e2$ from multiple relevant contexts. The notion of coverage criteria applies here as well. A test suite previously designed to cover a UI event $e2$ can be expanded to cover all possible occurrences of $e2$, for example.

As an example, consider the popular `Copy` $\rightarrow$ `Paste` operation common to many applications. `Paste` has no effect unless `Copy` has been performed; but once `Copy` has been performed correctly, a `Paste` event should have the effect of inserting any copied text. Going back further, we know that `Copy` only has an effect after text selection, and most applications only support text selection after text has been inserted or loaded, and so on.

1.5 Automated GUI Testing With Models

Testers must become domain experts to appropriately incorporate context while performing testing activities. If left as a purely manual exercise, important effects of context can easily be overlooked. If the same knowledge could be obtained and modeled in an automated way, some of these problems could potentially be avoided.

Researchers have made a great deal of progress over the last decade in the area of automated MBT of applications which are driven by a GUI. GUI-driven applications comprise a large subset of the broader group of event-driven applications considered so far. System-level testing of GUI-driven applications involves the execution of input events on the graphical interface—an activity commonly referred to as *GUI testing*. (Note that GUI-driven applications can be tested by a number of other means as well—at the Unit level, API level, etc.—but tests interacting with the GUI itself will be our focus here.)

1.5.1 GUI Testing

Fig. 3 shows a test case for the JabRef Reference Manager, an open-source Java Desktop application (http://jabref.sourceforge.net/). This test case involves (1) enabling the search panel, (2) entering a search term, (3) clicking to fetch results, and (4) selecting a result. Each of these steps corresponds to a

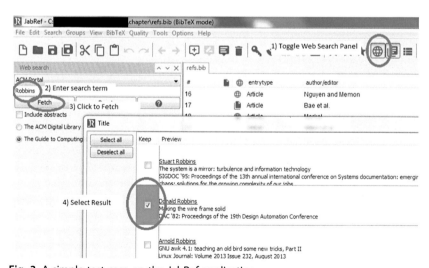

Fig. 3 A simple test case on the JabRef application.

single event in the test case (not considering yet any verifications to be performed). Consider several things about this test case:

- Events are associated with and performed on GUI controls (also known as *widgets*).
- Individual widgets typically support only a small set of actions. For example, the text box from step 2 supports text entry, while other widgets involved in the test do not allow text to be entered.
- Events may or may not require accompanying input data (as step 2 in this test case does).

Now let us consider verification. The use of a GUI by an application does not limit any non-GUI sources available for output verification (e.g., files produced by the application), but GUI-driven applications do introduce the GUI's state as an interesting subset of verifiable application state. At any point, we can verify the set of visible widgets (or any collection of properties on those widgets) to assert the state of the GUI as part of a test.

The type of verification being done (e.g., within a log file, GUI, database, etc.) determines the information needed to completely specify a test case. At a minimum, specification of each input step requires information necessary to identify widgets and perform events (including input data, if applicable). A number of popular industry tools can automatically replay well-specified test cases for GUI-driven applications in various domains (see Selenium WebDriver, Android Robotium, Quick Test Professional, and others). Each of these tools, however, depends on error-prone manual creation of test cases, and prior to that, manual test suite design, and maintenance decisions.

GUITAR is an automated, model-based alternative to capture/replay manual test case construction developed by researchers over the course of the past decade [6]. GUITAR's tools automatically construct event-based models of GUI applications, and generate test cases by traversing these models in ways that achieve predefined coverage criteria.

1.5.2 Existing Model-Based Approaches Which Incorporate Context

The standard GUITAR workflow builds an *event-flow* model of the application and generates a test suite which covers all event sequences of length 2 from the model. The event-flow model incorporates knowledge of *may-follow* relationships between events, where A *may-follow* indicates that an event B may be executed after an event A. Test suite generation algorithms use information about *may-follow* relationships to construct test cases and satisfy coverage criteria.

Additional methods derived from the event-flow model have also incorporated additional context information. The event-interaction graph (EIG) model enhances the event-flow model with information collected at runtime about the effects of event execution on underlying, non-GUI application state [7–9].

The Probabilistic Event-Flow Graph (PEFG) of Brooks and Memon augments the event-flow graph with probabilities according to event sequence collected from real users [10]. On a different domain, McMaster and Memon consider sequences of method call stacks to inform a reduction technique [11].

Model-based approaches defined on the GUI domain appear to be much more scalable than approaches defined directly on lower levels of application state. State-based test generation attempts to capture the entire application state [12–14], which has not proven scalable for event-driven applications. Similarly, data-flow approaches require analysis of statements of code [15, 16]. Neither method directly informs the general consideration of context in arbitrary domains.

Later in this chapter, I elaborate on additional model-based approaches more directly relevant to the new class of models I am introducing in Section 2.1, and on the specific modeling approaches relevant for regression models in Section 3.

1.6 Problems With Existing MBT Approaches

As I practicing software engineer, I have seen very little practical application of MBT. In my observation, MBT is not inapplicable. Teams of dedicated QA Engineers spend months developing effective test automation only to be prone to gaps in consideration of context. In my opinion, MBT in its current forms is often viewed as impractical because:

- MBT cannot really provide the very guarantees that it claims (such as coverage criteria and full automation).
- Model construction and verification are tedious.
- Exhaustive MBT approaches are too resource intensive to be practical.
- Model construction activities are seen as "reimplementing the application" rather than verifying its logic.

While the fourth problem above can be seen as more philosophical than practical (though it remains a real industry concern), the remaining three issues are directly addressed by the techniques presented in this chapter.

After presenting some additional background on MBT and GUI testing in Section 2, I describe in Section 3 a new class of models for MBT: predictive regression models. In an MBT workflow with a "feedback loop," the results from executing one subset of generated tests are used to inform the generation of additional tests. Predictive regression models for MBT use a subset of test execution results from a feedback loop to construct a predictive model rather than simply updating an existing structural or behavioral model.

The predictive model can then predict for each subsequent generated test case whether its inclusion in the resulting suite of tests is likely to cause problems. In this way, predictive regression models can reduce the likelihood of producing test cases which do not actually contribute to a given coverage criteria, or which are likely to have problems being executed in general (just as two examples).

In Section 5, I describe a regression model for test case feasibility as one example of a predictive regression model applied to MBT. I walk through the construction of this model, and the identification of features, to show that it was effective in identifying infeasible test cases (that is, test cases that were not completely executable).

The research presented in Section 5 is only possible due to addressing the scalability problem presented as the third problem above. To that end, I describe a parallel execution framework for MBT in Section 4, which I believe shows one way to make MBT approaches for GUI testing more practical. The execution framework uses state-of-the-art technologies for automated test execution and containerization to make the most of available computing resources.

2. BACKGROUND

Before defining complementary predictive regression models for MBT, it is useful to consider existing research in MBT and GUI testing. This background lays the groundwork for considering a fully automated MBT workflow for model-based GUI testing, which has an extensive line of existing academic research and provides interesting applications for predictive regression models.

2.1 Model-Based Testing

Modeling has become essential for modern software development. Developers now have models for many things: models of the Software Development Life Cycle (SDLC), such as Waterfall or Spiral; models that formalize a system's requirements; models of a system's objects or runtime components; and models for every phase of the SDLC. The goal of modeling systems is usually abstraction. For example, during software requirements gathering activities, stakeholders do not care about the implementation details of the system. They can abstract these details away by modeling only the user and the system as a whole. As development of any one feature moves through the SDLC, different models abstract away less relevant details from the task at hand. Often, multiple models—each emphasizing different software characteristics—are needed in order to effectively make decisions.

As I assert Section 1, effective software testing depends on the ability to incorporate relevant context. Uniformly, all consideration of context requires the presence of some type of "model" of the application. Even in cases where a formal abstraction is not defined, a domain expert's own mental model is driving testing activities. Researchers have predominantly proposed three classes of models capable of considering context and drive testing activities, all of which can be applied to event-based applications: state based, data flow, and event flow. Understanding these existing classes informs our new class of predictive regression models.

2.1.1 State-Based and Data-Flow Models

In state-based models of testing, testers construct state machine models which attempt to model an application in terms of its runtime states. Test case generation, then, attempts to satisfy various coverage criteria defined on the state machine. Though referred to by various names in the literature, coverage of transitions or *edges* in the model is a commonly used criteria [12–14]. Note that coverage of transitions requires the consideration of a single-length history of prior state. The event-driven domain of protocol testing was in many respects a catalyst for state-based testing approaches in the early 1990s [17, 18], though protocols considered at that time were much simpler domains than the event-driven protocols of today's applications.

In practice, automated construction of state machine models of nontrivial applications is often infeasible, despite a number of enhancements which attempt to limit the number of states and transitions that must be captured by the model. Cheng and Krishnakumar describe the Extended Finite State Machine (EFSM), which limits states by adding additional counters and runtime components [19]. Similarly, Shehady and Siewiorek describe an extension of FSMs to use variables, which limits the number of states to be explored [20], and the work of White *et al.* suggests subdividing models into usage-specific categories [21, 22].

In practice, these techniques provide some utility in well-defined or highly critical domains, but would likely be ineffective in the more complex domains of larger event-driven systems. In addition to the high cost of model construction at the often hidden and complex level of application states, the task of mapping back to a concrete, executable input domain remains an error-prone manual exercise.

In contrast to control-flow models, data-flow models of software track context by following traces of variables in a program. A model known as a *control-flow graph* details the flow of a program through its executable statements. The primary indicators of context are the uses of variables. Variable reads and writes and their use in interesting combinations are analyzed. Rapps and Weyuker first introduced a set of adequacy criteria for data-flow testing [15], focusing primarily on coverage of their Def/Use program graph. Frankl and Weyuker later expanded on these original criteria, claiming that many programs could not satisfy the central criteria of the original work [16], for reasons as common as a simple `for` loop. In practice, once again, reliable construction of program graphs and generation of tests which satisfy these criteria do not scale to the complexities of modern applications.

2.1.2 Event-Flow Models

Given the issues with state-based and data-flow approaches, Memon proposed the event-flow model for GUI testing [23, 24]. In this work, the nodes in a graphical model of the GUI capture behavioral *may-follow* relationships. Given the event-flow model, coverage criteria can be defined which consider the coverage of the *may-follow* relationships present in a GUI [25]. Important coverage criteria include pairwise coverage (covering all edges in the event-flow model's graph) and a more generic sequence-length coverage concept, which requires covering all sequences of events in the graph of a given length. (Note that pairwise coverage is a length-2 version of this criterion.) The event-flow model also applies to event-based applications more generically, and not strictly GUI-based applications.

Because test case construction considerations follow the construction of the event-flow model, the accuracy of the model determines the accuracy of any inferred and generated test cases. Given an accurate model, automatically generated test cases will be executable. Given an inaccurate model, infeasible test cases (i.e., those which cannot be completely executed) will be produced. The model has additional limitations due to its inference from structural and behavioral properties. It does not, for example, natively incorporate any information about code coverage or additional coverage criteria from non-GUI domains.

Fig. 4 shows a portion of the GUI and two models of the JabRef application: an intermediate model known as a "GUI Tree" and a derived event-flow model. Nodes in the event-flow model's graph represent events in the application's GUI, and the presence of edges in the model indicates that an event can successfully follow another. While most buttons are always available from any other, the Yes button is only available after clicking "Exit," because this button confirms the Exit operation. This relationship is evident in the event-flow model as well, as the corresponding edge between these nodes is missing.

Memon et al. later developed a reverse engineering tool known as the Ripper for constructing event-flow models in an automated way [26], giving this model some advantages over the previously discussed models. The fully automated approach constructs the GUI Tree model shown above, as an intermediate representation between the application GUI and the event-flow model. Automated model construction makes construction of models of modern GUI applications possible, for the first time. More recent work with the event-flow model has enhanced the model to focus on events more likely to find faults. To identify these events, automated testing workflows collect runtime information during test execution. Data collected during one execution can be reused to improve the model used in the next, and this process repeated iteratively [7–9]. The work of Yuan et al. explicitly aimed to consider events in context [27] based on the application of covering arrays to an adaptation of the event-flow model called the EIG.

2.2 GUI Testing

Since the start of the 21st century, GUI testing as a subdiscipline of software testing research has continued to grow significantly alongside the rise in the popularity of GUI-driven applications. Researchers often focus on MBT of GUI-driven applications, though industrial trends have yet to follow. This disconnect was also noted in a recent systematic mapping of published literature on the topic of GUI testing by Banerjee et al. [28].

One practical line of research which followed from the event-flow model was the Daily Automated Regression Testing (DART) framework [29], which was shown to be effective for identifying bugs which caused crashes in daily or nightly builds. The DART tools would later become

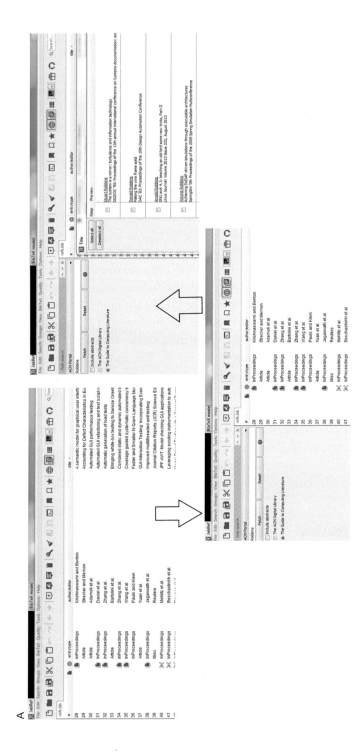

Fig. 4 Partial (A) GUI, (B) GUIStructure, and (C) EFG of the JabRef application.

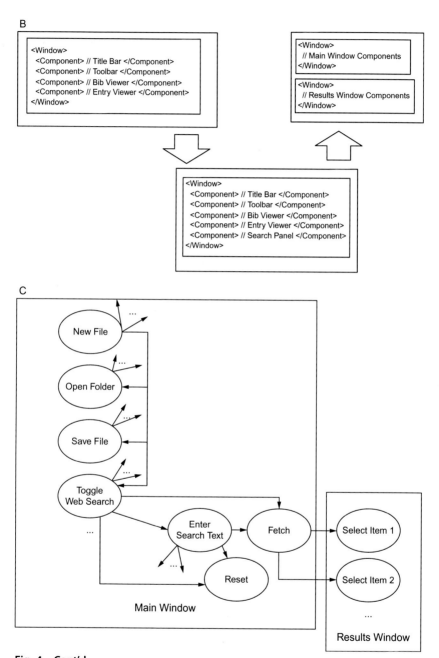

Fig. 4—Cont'd

the GUI Test Automation Framework (GUITAR), an open-source framework[a] for end-to-end automated testing on various GUI application platforms. I consider GUITAR in much greater detail throughout the remainder of this chapter.

In 2013, Nguyen *et al.* published an updated description of GUITAR from an architectural perspective [6], carrying out a number of case studies which highlighted some of the pitfalls of the automated model-based approach. Most objections arose from the reverse engineering Ripper tool, due to difficulties with widget identification and the simplicity of its algorithm (which executes in a single application instance). The authors observed that the one-time execution of the Ripper led to invalid model construction due to the effects of event and application context. Incomplete or otherwise incorrect models lead to the generation of infeasible test cases. This *infeasibility problem* is exactly what I use predictive regression models to address in Section 5.

2.2.1 Test Oracles

Another important characteristic of testing approaches is test oracle support. By "test oracle," I mean the method of verification for a test. One long-standing problem with GUI testing is the cost of maintaining a set of expected values to be verified during test execution. As far back as 1992, Richardson *et al.* studied the challenges of oracles for event-based systems (referring to these systems as *reactive systems*) [30, 31].

More recently, Memon *et al.* began to look at oracles for GUIs [32]. Xie and Memon carried out a large-scale empirical study with GUITAR that showed the utility of more advanced oracles over crash testing [33]. Examples of other more effective oracles in that study include those defined on the GUI structure to be checked during test execution.

When considering predictive regression models defined after test case execution, test execution artifacts that traditionally act as inputs to oracles can also be inputs to predictive models constructed after test execution. If each test case has some N corresponding execution artifacts, these artifacts may come from any number of domains. For example, a GUI test case may produce a console log as one artifact, a sequence of GUI structures captured during replay as another, a sequence of calls stacks as another, a sequence of lines of code as another, and so on.

---

[a] http://guitar.sf.net.

In the case of test oracles, testers collect artifacts with the goal of applying verifications. In the broader case of constructing predictive models, we may obviously have other goals, such as addressing potential problems with test case feasibility, test coverage, or other factors.

2.3 Summary

The remainder of this chapter builds on this academic and industry background for MBT and GUI testing. As I suggest in Section 1, MBT approaches have real problems that keep them from being generally applicable. The background presented here further highlights these limitations and places the construction of predictive regression models within the context of existing work. It also further motivates our construction of an improved fully automated model-based workflow in the following sections.

3. A WORKFLOW FOR PREDICTIVE MODELING

In this section, I consider one well-documented, fully automated MBT approach, and how this approach can be extended and improved with predictive regression models.

3.1 The GUITAR Standard Workflow

A number of existing studies have leveraged the GUITAR framework for automated MBT [6]. Fig. 5 shows GUITAR's sequence-length test case

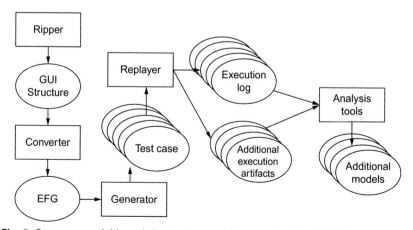

Fig. 5 Common model-based GUI testing workflow enabled by GUITAR.

generation workflow (which we referred to as the "standard workflow" in the 2013 paper cited above).

At a high level, a reverse engineering tool called the Ripper produces a model called a GUI Tree, which represents the structure of the GUI as observed during the reverse engineering (aka "ripping") process. This GUI Tree output is called a GUIStructure. A Converter tool then converts the GUIStructure into an Event-flow Graph (EFG), by inferring behavioral relationships of the application from the GUIStructure. The Generator tool traverses the EFG to output many executable test cases. Finally, the Replayer tool executes each test case (one at a time).

There are a number of configuration options for this workflow. To keep things simple (and comparable with existing published studies), I will assume default algorithms for each tool for the sake of this chapter. For test case generation, I assume the Random Sequence-Length strategy for the Generator tool.

As Fig. 5 indicates, each tool in this workflow outputs one or more arti-facts, which in turn drive the next tool and step in the workflow. I describe the key tools of a "standard workflow" for automated MBT in the following sections. I use a running example of the JabRef application shown in Fig. 4.

3.1.1 A Note About Application Platform
GUITAR's oldest and most frequently cited tools are based on the Java Foundation Classes (JFC)[b] and the Swing UI components. Importantly, however, only the Ripper and Replayer have platform-specific compo-nents. While the core algorithms for ripping and replaying are shared across platforms, these tools do need to know how to interact with the GUIs of a specific platform. The Converter and Generator tools, as well as any tools we may consider for constructing predictive regression models, are not platform specific.

This is not to say that application platform would not impact modeling whatsoever. As we might expect, an event-based behavioral model from a mobile application will look significantly different from the same model extracted from a Web or Java desktop application. These differences may indeed affect the richness of any predictive models derived later in the workflow; but they should not affect, for example, the accuracy of those models relative to their inputs.

---

[b] https://docs.oracle.com/javase/tutorial/uiswing/start/about.html.

3.1.2 The GUI Ripper

GUITAR's standard workflow starts by leveraging an implementation of the GUI Ripping technique [34]. Through GUI ripping, GUITAR's Ripper tool automatically constructs a model of the GUI of an application. The Ripper takes as input a number of parameters related to launching the application and guiding the ripping process. The output of the Ripper is a single GUIStructure file, which captures the windows and widgets the Ripper encountered.

Importantly, GUITAR's default Ripper uses only a single pass through an application, attempting to "rip" as many windows and widgets as possible recursively before exiting and producing a consolidated GUIStructure. Fig. 6 contains pseudocode for the ripping algorithm, adapted from the version presented by Banerjee *et al.* [34]. A hypothetical ideal Ripper would require potentially infinite passes through the application (e.g., to capture every event in every possible context).

3.1.3 Ripper Algorithm

Walking through the algorithm as applied to the running example from Fig. 4, get-top-level-windows would initially a single window (the Main window of the JabRef application). The Ripper would then call RIP-RECURSIVE to extract the widgets and properties from this window, and identify and interact with each widget. Upon interacting with Toggle

---

PROCEDURE RIP (SUT A)	
T = get-top-level-windows(A)	1
$GUI = T$	2
FORALL $t \in T$ DO	3
RIP-RECURSIVE(t)	4
PROCEDURE RIP-RECURSIVE (Window t)	
Ψ = extract-widgets-and-properties(t)	5
ϵ = identity-executable-widgets(Ψ)	6
FORALL $e \in \epsilon$ DO	7
execute(e)	8
C = get-invoked-windows(e)	9
t = extract-widgets-and-properties(t)	10
GUI = merge(GUI, C)	11
FORALL $c \in C$ DO	12
RIP-RECURSIVE(c)	13

Fig. 6 Pseudocode for the Ripper.

Web Search button, the new Search panel and its widgets would additionally be extracted and recursively inspected as well. Upon interacting with the "Fetch" button, the Results Window would be discovered. The final result is a GUIStructure with at least two windows, each with several widgets and properties.

One complexity not immediately obvious from the pseudocode is the identification and utilization of terminal widgets. Upon launch, the Ripper takes a list of terminal widgets properties as a configuration option. The algorithm excludes any widgets with these properties from the return values of identify-executable-widgets. For the sake of simplicity, the pseudocode also omits the algorithm's execution of terminal widgets as needed to exit windows (i.e., once all other executable events have been executed). get-invoked-windows also detects closed windows, in the case that a window was closed by the execution of an event unexpectedly.

3.1.4 Configuration Options and Customizations

As we note in the 2013 paper [6], the Ripper is very sensitive to configuration and customization, such as the configuration of terminal and ignored widgets. Many existing studies with GUITAR use very basic configurations for terminal and ignored widgets (e.g., treating "Ok," "Cancel," and other common exit buttons as terminal widgets for all applications). In any practical application of the GUITAR workflow, the GUIStructure output by the Ripper must be inspected and validated for completeness. Since the output of the Ripper drives the rest of the workflow, this validation and configuration cycle is critical.

For example, assume that a terminal widget is missing from the Ripper's configuration. This omission would cause the Ripper algorithm to treat the terminal widget as it would any other widget in the application, causing one or more windows to exit prior to having extracted all possible information. This would lead to a less accurate, smaller GUIStructure in terms of widgets and properties.

As another example of the impact of Ripper customizations, in our 2013 paper we describe customization of the Ripper and Replayer to deal with custom widget types [6]. These customizations lead to a much better discovery of the application's GUI, as more windows, widgets, and properties are discovered. In turn, the GUIStructure produced by the Ripper's algorithm from Fig. 6 is a much more accurate model of the application, in that it covers much more of the GUI's components. Lacking such customizations, the Ripping algorithm extracts fewer windows, widgets, and properties and effectively *skips over* the missed components altogether, as the algorithm makes clear. The custom components (and any children) will be completely absent from the GUIStructure.

As with choice of platform, the configuration and customization options for the Ripper impact the consideration of predictive regression models in the sense that the accuracy and richness of the GUIStructure impact the relative accuracy and richness of any derived models. We can still construct predictive regression models from smaller (and possibly inaccurate) GUIStructure models—in fact, as I suggest later in the chapter, we can use predictive regression models to directly address issues with accuracy.

3.1.5 Event Properties

The most important pieces of information extracted by the Ripper are related to an application's events. Structurally, each Window in the GUI has one or more Components, where Components can be Widgets (which are interactive) or groups of Components (which are collections of other components or Widgets). For example, a Menu is a Component in this paradigm. A Menu Button (which is clickable) is a Widget. Widgets subsequently have events, and each event has properties. Most properties are structural, but two key computed properties are also essential to downstream processing:

- *Event ID*: a unique ID for the event, created as a hash of the properties from the widget and its parent window.
- *Event type*: an inferred category for the event, based on observed effects on the GUI after execution.

Both the EFG and executable test cases use the event ID as a unique identifier. The ID is computed rather than random to assist the Ripper's own algorithm in avoiding infinite loops of property extraction (e.g., in the get-invoked-windows method referred to from the pseudocode), and to keep IDs consistent across otherwise identical executions of the Ripper. Because the IDs are based on a hash, any difference in structural properties (e.g., the width, height, or screen location) of the widget will cause it to be considered a new widget for inclusion in the GUIStructure.

The event type in this context refers to the effects this event has on the GUI. (To be clear, it does not refer to clicking, typing, or any other *type* of events which can be carried out on a widget.) There are five event types, each of which has a specific interpretation in the event-flow model produced by the Converter in the next workflow step [24]:

- *menu-open*: an event which caused a menu to open.
- *termination*: an event which caused a window to close.
- *restricted-focus*: an event which caused a window to open, if the opened window blocked access to all existing windows.
- *unrestricted-focus*: an event which caused a window to open, if the opened window did not block access to existing windows.
- *system-interaction*: an event which did not cause any apparent change to the GUI.

After computing these values, the GUIStructure contains all necessary information for downstream workflow steps.

3.1.6 Conversion

The next two steps in the standard GUITAR workflow work from model representations rather than directly with applications. As the next step, the Converter converts the GUIStructure model into a Directed Graph called the EFG [24]. The EFG has GUI events as nodes. Edges in the EFG represent presumed relationships between GUI events. In particular, the EFG captures *may-follow* relations between events in the GUI. If an event e_2 has a connection from event e_1 in the EFG, e_2 should be immediately executable after the execution of e_1.

As the transition from GUI Tree to EFG in Fig. 4 shows, the EFG abstracts away all information except for events and their relationships. The conversion from GUI information to event relationships is purely structural, based solely on the information available in the GUIStructure. The XML representation of the EFG includes event IDs, *initial* flags for each event, and a matrix representation of the graph itself.

Fig. 7 shows pseudocode for the primary algorithm used in computing the EFG, which computes *may-follow* relations for a given event. (This figure adapted from Memon's original algorithm presented in Ref. [24].) Specifically, this algorithm computes the set of events which *may-follow* a given event v. As mentioned earlier, this algorithm depends on the computed Event Type present in the GUIStructure for each event.

For each event type, the algorithm uses the relationships captured in the GUIStructure to compute the events available from the current event. The

```
PROCEDURE GET-FOLLOWS (VERTEX V)
  W = window(v); B = top-level-events(W)                          1
  IF EventType(v) == menu-open                                    2
    IF v ∈ B                                                      3
      return(MenuChoices(v) ∪ { v } ∪ B                          4
    ELSE                                                          5
      return(MenuChoices(v) ∪ { v } ∪ follows(parent(v))         6
  IF EventType(v) == system-interaction                          7
    return(B)                                                     8
  IF EventType(v) == termination                                 9
    return(top-level-events(invoker(W)))                         10
  IF EventType(v) == unrestricted-focus                          11
    return(B ∪ top-level-events(invoked(v)))                     12
  IF EventType(v) == restricted-focus                            13
    return(top-level-events(invoked(v)))                         14
```

Fig. 7 Pseudocode for computing *may-follow* relationships from an event.

logic for each case depends on the event type's effects on the GUI, with limitations introduced as windows and menus are opened and closed. system-interaction events were observed to have no effect on the GUI during ripping and likewise can be followed by any events which were available before their execution.

The events available after executing a menu-open event depend on whether the event is available at the top level of its window. For example, if a user must click a File menu in order to click Save, the user can click File within its own window at any time; but Save can only be clicked once File is expanded. The File case is line 3 in the pseudocode, and the Save case is line 5.

For events which invoke new windows (unrestricted-focus and restricted-focus), the events which may follow depend on the nature of the window invoked. If the window invoked was *modal*, meaning that it blocked interaction with all other windows, then only events in the new window may follow. If the window was not modal, then the events in the new window as well as any events already available may still follow.

Events in the EFG are also marked with an *initial* value, which indicates whether each event can be executed immediately after application start as a value of true or false. All events available from the root windows of the application have this flag set to *true*, and all others have a value of *false*.

3.1.7 Test Case Generation

Next, the Test Case Generator traverses the EFG to generate test cases. The Generator takes as input the EFG produced by the Converter and generation parameters. GUITAR's basic libraries support multiple test case generation strategies. One popular choice for test case generation is the "random sequence-length" test case generator, which randomly selects a given number of test cases from a much larger pool of test cases defined on a criteria of sequence-length coverage.

The Generator outputs one file per each requested test case, which I refer to as the "test case input file." Each file specifies the sequence of events which define the test case. Even for short, constant sequence lengths, tests can include a varying number of steps. The test case input files include all information needed to perform the events. For all events, an event and widget identifier (ID) is needed. When entering text, the text is needed. In GUITAR's case, additional inputs are configurable, though the vast majority of existing studies with GUITAR use mouse clicks only.

Fig. 8 includes pseudocode for the sequence-length test case generation algorithm. Given a sequence length L, the algorithm generates one test case for each sequence of length L in the EFG. Sequences up to length L are identified by walking forward from each node up to length L, then a "path to root" is prefixed onto each sequence. The pathToRoot method walks backward from a given vertex (i.e., the first vertex in the sequence being covered) until reaching an event which has an *initial* flag set to *true*.

We can also introduce random sampling to test suites produced by the sequence-length generation algorithm after the algorithm completes, by

---

```
PROCEDURE SEQUENCE-LENGTH-TESTS (EFG G, LENGTH L)
  for v ∈ vertices(G)                                                1
  S = S ∪ GENERATE-SEQUENCES(L, v)                                   2
PROCEDURE GENERATE-SEQUENCES (LENGTH L, SEQUENCE POSTFIX)
  IF L == 1                                                          3
    P = pathToRoot(first(POSTFIX))                                   4
    writeTest(P, POSTFIX)                                            5
  ELSE                                                               6
    for v ∈ successors(last(POSTFIX))                                7
      NP = concat(POSTFIX, v)                                        8
      GENERATE-SEQUENCES(L - 1, NP)                                  9
```

Fig. 8 Pseudocode for sequence-length test case generation.

choosing a random set of indices from the entire pool of available tests. This allows test suites to be derived from a richer set of events and event relationships (i.e., from exhaustive test suites designed to cover longer-length subsequences) without requiring exhaustive execution of every single test case. This information gathered from a more complete set of events can be a significant advantage when constructing predictive regression models

3.1.8 Test Case Replay

After generation of test cases, the workflow includes execution of the generated test cases with the GUITAR Replayer tool. As a piece of software, the Replayer tool is very similar to the Ripper: a platform-specific tool with event and widget awareness. The Replayer, though, simply takes a single Test Case, EFG, and GUIStructure as input and executes the steps from the Test Case in sequence.

The Replayer only directly outputs a text log of execution results. Most researchers of MBT approaches collect additional output artifacts from the application during test case execution, in order to apply a more interesting test oracle [33]. As discussed in more detail later, we also derive predictive regression models from these execution artifacts.

3.2 Adding Predictive Regression Models

To this point, I have described the use of models to extract and process GUI information and to generate test cases. As presented so far, the model-based workflow still exhibits a number of the problems outlined in Section 1. We can now add additional steps that incorporate predictive regression models to improve on the overall utility of MBT workflows.

3.2.1 MBT Problems That Predictive Regression Models Can Address

I propose that MBT workflows such as the workflow of GUITAR presented in this chapter can incorporate predictive regression models as follows:

- Add a feedback loop, such that test case execution results are used to improve the generated test cases themselves, producing progressively "better" test suites until desired criteria are met.
- Construct predictive regression models from randomly sampled batches of test case execution results and use these models to classify newly proposed test cases prior to their execution.

In machine learning terms, I am proposing here the use of supervised learning to solve "classification problems." Tying this back to the MBT problems I have mentioned thus far, I suggest that even the simplest case of binary classification can be leveraged to detect problems such as test case infeasibility and duplicate test coverage.

In the case of test case feasibility, we can learn from a set of executed test cases the features of test cases which tend to become infeasible. We use a learned set of application-specific features to filter out newly proposed test cases before even executing them. I describe a model for test case feasibility and show data indicating the effectiveness of this approach in Section 5.

In the case of test case coverage, we can learn from a set of executed test cases the features of test cases which actually correspond with desired coverage criteria. Note that coverage in this sense can come from any domain: GUI event coverage, code coverage, call stack coverage, coverage of HTTP or database calls, or any other feasible domain. In this case, the key element in learning a model would be obtaining the right test execution artifacts and then extracting the right "features" from these artifacts. While I do not explore coverage modeling in this chapter, the work of McMaster and Memon [11] explores this link in the area of call stack coverage and implies its generalization.

Consider how the proposed predictive regression models compare to the typical models in MBT workflows. While the existing models are structural (such as the GUIStructure) and behavioral (such as the EFG), the new predictive regression models can be defined on any domain. While the existing models may ultimately drive test case generation, the predictive models can act as a filter for generated test cases, whether or not their feedback leads to any adjustments in structural or behavioral models. In Section 5, I elaborate on a few existing alternatives for addressing the infeasibility problem through updates to structural and behavioral models, which offers a concrete example of this contrast.

3.2.2 Supervised Learning and Binary Classification

Machine learning involves the use of computers to learn patterns from data. In practical applications, the learned patterns are often used to predict something about the nature of unseen data. Within the context of predictive regression models, we want to predict some attribute of a test case prior to its execution. We provide a test case as input to the machine learning algorithm, and expect to receive a prediction (e.g., feasible or infeasible) as output. This type of problem is known as a binary classification: classification because I want to categorize the input, and binary because there are only two categories of the predicted value.

A machine learning technique such as binary classification requires at least two complementary algorithms that work in separate phases. During a *training* phase, one algorithm fits a statistical model based on a set of inputs. After training, a separate algorithm can use the trained statistical model to predict outcomes given previously unseen inputs. Mathematically, these algorithms operate on numerically coded *features* of input data, where each feature maps to an input variable X_i in the underlying statistical model. Algorithms that also know the correct output category of an input during training are known as *supervised* (as opposed to *unsupervised* techniques, which do not know the output category of inputs during training). In the case of predictive regression models for MBT, we can assume that outputs will be labeled (though there are surely some interesting applications for unsupervised models in MBT that we will not explore here).

3.2.3 Generalized Linear Model

Above, I explain that binary classification requires fitting a statistical model during training, then using that model to make predictions. Assuming a set of p features X_j used to predict an outcome $\hat{Y}$, a linear model is one that estimates Y as:

$$\hat{Y} = \hat{\beta}_0 + \sum_{j=1}^{p} X_j \hat{\beta}_j \tag{1}$$

Under this model, training involves solving an optimization problem that chooses the coefficients $\hat{\beta}$ that lead to the best approximations for $\hat{y}$. After training, predictions can be made by simply summing the $X_i\hat{\beta}$ terms from the features of a previously unseen data point. The $\hat{\beta}_0$ added to every prediction is known as the *intercept* of the model. The intercept may also be added to the model by modeling an extra feature term X_0, which always has a value of 1. From the remainder of this section, I assume that formulation for simplicity.

The *Generalized Linear Model* or GLM [35] provides a general formulation of the model described earlier. The GLM formulation makes three fairly general assumptions:

1. Outcomes are assumed to come from a probability distribution function, from a broad class of certain acceptable forms with parameters θ and ϕ.
2. Predictions are made with a linear predictor η (i.e., the linear combination of X_j and $\hat{\beta}_j$ given above).
3. A *link* function g provides an estimate for the parameter θ of the probability distribution function, given labeled training data.

Under this formulation, estimating the parameters $\hat{\beta}_j$ means solving an optimization problem, which minimizes the difference between the observed and predicted values for Y. The original authors of the GLM showed an expectation maximization formulation of this model fitting which works for all GLMs [35]. The training problem can also be expressed in terms of a loss function defined on Y and $\hat{Y}$:

$$\min_{\hat{\beta}} \ell(Y, \hat{Y}) \qquad (2)$$

The acceptable forms of the probability distribution function include the very broad exponential family of probability distribution functions, including the well-known normal, gamma, and binomial distribution functions, among many others. The simplest and most common form of GLM is linear regression, which assumes a normal distribution and only requires the identity function as its linking function. For binary classification problems, logistic regression provides more robust performance than linear regression by adding some additional constraints.

Formulated as a GLM, logistic regression uses a binomial distribution and *logistic* function as a loss function. Logistic regression makes sense for binary classification problems because its predicted values are defined on a range from 0 to 1. Further, the shape of the logistic function more easily fits data that prefer values at exactly 0 and 1.

3.2.4 Adding Regularization With Lasso

As described thus far, our predictive regression models for MBT could use logistic regression over a set of available features to fit a model given a set of test execution artifacts as training data. In practice, this model would quickly encounter issues with convergence and would tend to *overfit* the training data, especially when the number of training examples (in our case, the number of test cases) is much less than the number of features in the training data.

To counter these problems, we could add more test executions to the training data; but test execution is expensive, and adding tests would tend to add more features until a very large number of (e.g., hundreds of thousands or more) tests were in the training set. Regularized models provide a more stable alternative. Revisiting the loss function formulation of the GLM from the above, regularized models add a new term to the optimization problem:

$$\min_{\hat{\beta}} \ell(Y, \hat{Y}) + \lambda R(\hat{\beta}) \tag{3}$$

A metaparameter λ accompanies the new term, meaning that there will now be many models to choose from given the same training data—one model for each value of λ. We now need to add an additional step after model fitting to choose the value of λ which offers the best model.

Cross-validation on the training data allows us to compare the relative fit of each model. When applying cross-validation, we divide training data into a fixed number N of randomly selected groups (say, 5 or 10). We then train a set of models across our values of λ using only $N - 1$ of the N groups and compare how the model performs when trying to predict the labels of the last (Nth) group. We then choose the model that performs best on some preselected metric (typically, but not necessarily, the model that makes the fewest errors in prediction). In Section 5, I provide a concrete example of selecting the best λ value for feasibility models.

There are multiple options for the regularization function R above, which should cause the optimization to prefer the simplest possible model (i.e., with the lowest amount of "mass" spread across estimated coefficients). If possible, coefficients should also be allowed to reduce to 0 in the model, so that they may be ignored altogether.

Tibshirani formalized the use of an ℓ_1 norm as a regularization term, which he called the "least absolute shrinkage and selection operator" or "Lasso" [36]. The ℓ_1 norm is given by taking the sum of the absolute values of the coefficients:

$$R = ||\hat{\beta}||_1 = \sum_{j=1}^{p} |\hat{\beta}_j| \tag{4}$$

As the name suggests, use of this term for regularization does allow for both shrinkage of coefficients and selection of parameters, by allowing unimportant coefficients to have estimates of 0. More recently, Friedman *et al.* provide a very fast solver for the Lasso optimization problem known as `glmnet` [37]. They also provide an R package with this implementation, which supports both linear and logistic regression (among many other options). I provide scripts for constructing binary classifiers using logistic regression from `glmnet` in Section 5.

3.2.5 Modeling Summary

To summarize, I find that the following approaches offer the most immediate benefit for predictive regression models in MBT workflows: binary classifiers trained through supervised learning with Lasso-regularized logistic regression as the underlying statistical model. With this same foundation, we can construct binary classifiers for nearly any test case feature that can be extracted from execution artifacts. As long as we are able to identify test case features that correlate with our predictions, we can count on the regularization to minimize and even deselect the features that are not contributing.

4. A SCALABLE FRAMEWORK FOR EXECUTION

Carrying out a large-scale empirical study of testing techniques requires a robust execution infrastructure. To support large-scale MBT studies in general, and the consideration of predictive regression models in particular (as these models further drive up the number of test case executions required in MBT workflows), I require the following of an execution infrastructure:

- *Portable*: The infrastructure should be adaptable to any group of Linux machines.
- *Persistent*: The infrastructure should support persistence and easy backup and restore operations for input and output artifacts.
- *Configurable*: The infrastructure should support fully automated backup and restore of all machine configurations.
- *Compatible*: The infrastructure should support execution of arbitrary Java tools and R scripts.
- *Parallel*: The infrastructure should support the execution of many GUI test cases simultaneously.

In this section, I present a state-of-the-art framework for executing MBT workflows across clusters of Linux machines such as those available from popular cloud providers. I also elaborate on the construction of predictive regression models within this framework, providing sample scripts for the modeling techniques discussed so far.

4.1 Overview

Fig. 9 shows the core runtime components of the infrastructure I have developed which achieves these goals, and dependencies between those components. I use Docker[c] to develop virtual machine images to automate the configuration of every infrastructure component. Each of the five infrastructure components in Fig. 9 has a corresponding Docker component (called an "image" at build time, and a "container" at runtime), precisely describing its creation and configuration.

Each task to be performed within a workflow is automated via a Jenkins CI[d] job. The Jenkins Master controls the execution of automated jobs, and actual execution of commands occurs in completely separate "slave" containers. Before each job finishes, artifacts are persisted to one of a MongoDB[e] database or the Apache Maven[f] Java library repository (MongoDB for test execution and experiment artifacts, and Maven Repo for compiled code artifacts).

The Jenkins Master, MongoDB, and Maven Repo components use existing open-source tools directly off the shelf (Jenkins CI, MongoDB, and Sonatype Nexus,[g] respectively). The Job Execution Slave components use open-source tools such as the GUITAR Java toolchain, Gradle, and R to carry out the specifics of the MBT workflows such as those we have considered in this chapter. I elaborate on the use of Docker to configure each of these infrastructure components (including two separate types of Job Execution Slaves) in Section 4.2.

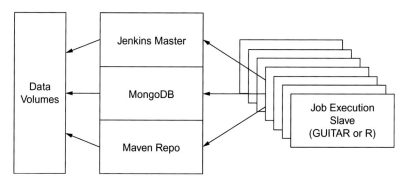

Fig. 9 Infrastructure components and dependencies.

---

[c] https://www.docker.com/.
[d] https://www.jenkins-ci.org/.
[e] https://www.mongodb.org/.
[f] https://maven.apache.org/.
[g] http://www.sonatype.org/nexus/.

Persistence of experiment artifacts requires the development of a new tool, which I call TestData. I use this tool from within Job Execution Slave components during job execution to persist artifacts as appropriate. I describe the implementation of this tool in Section 4.4.

Jenkins CI natively supports execution of automated jobs, including concurrent execution of jobs in separate Job Execution Slaves. However, coordinating batches of parallel jobs requires custom code using the HTTP API provided by the Jenkins Master. I elaborate on my use of Jenkins CI jobs and my approach for parallel job execution in Section 4.5.

When constructing predictive regression models, I make extensive use of R,[h] an open-source platform for statistics and graphics. I elaborate on a number of custom R scripts (which make heavy use of third-party libraries) in Section 5.5.

4.2 Portable Configurations With Docker

Docker is an open-source tool for defining and running software within containers, which "sandbox processes from each other [38]." Docker containers represent a lighter-weight virtualization alternative as compared to traditional virtual machines (VMs). The containers also make use of shared, read-only copies of file systems to optimize disk usage. Ultimately, however, the processes running within containers consume at least the same amount of resources (CPU, Memory, File I/O, and otherwise) as the same processes would consume if run on the host operating system directly.

In terms of platform support, Docker runs on the majority of Linux platforms and inside of Linux VMs on other host operating systems. Moving my infrastructure components and their configuration to Docker images allows for replication of those components on any available hardware running a native Linux operating system or VM, as required.

To use Docker, this framework follows this life cycle:

1. (Optional) Build a Docker *image* based on a customized script called a Dockerfile.[i]

2. Given an image ID and runtime properties such as *mapped data volumes*, *ports*, and *environment variables*, start a Docker container.

3. When done using the container, manually stop.

---

[h] https://www.r-project.org/.
[i] The full Dockerfile spec at time of this framework's construction is available online at https://docs.docker.com/v1.8/reference/builder/.

The broader Docker ecosystem also readily supports quick and reliable use of existing, publicly provided container images. The Docker Hub[j] indexes a full set of publicly available container images and allows them to easily be "pulled" onto a machine via the Docker command-line interface (CLI). The images on the Docker Hub are open source so that their configuration can be completely inspected prior to use or enhancement. Container images support inheritance as well so that images based on publicly available configurations can be further customized for particular use cases.

In this framework, I leverage five unique Docker images, as shown in Table 2. Docker images can be extended at build time to install and configure additional tools and can also be configured to use mounted file system locations called volumes. The Contents and Volumes columns describe at a high level the Dockerfile enhancements and volume usage leveraged by each container, respectively.

Data volumes also play a critical role in the usage of Docker for this framework. Docker images include a snapshot of the entire file system at creation time. For "always-on," data-backed components which we would like to efficiently backup and restore from, full persistence at the image level would require a great deal of disk space, versioning, and other additional engineering overhead.

Alternatively, Docker provides options for mounting data into containers at runtime rather than baking data into images at image creation time. When Docker containers are started, local file system locations from the server which is running Docker can be mapped to a container's file system. Also, containers can be configured at runtime to inherit all volume mappings from any already running container.

Table 2 Docker Images

Name	Contents	Volumes
Jenkins Master	Jenkins Master Web app	Job artifacts, configuration files
MongoDB	Database Master	Data directory
Maven Repo	Artifact repository	Jar files, index
GUITAR Slave	Jenkins agent, GUITAR tools, Subject applications	None
R Slave	Jenkins agent, R, R packages	None

---

[j] https://hub.docker.com/.

I leverage these features to create and populate a "data container" with all required data volumes included. With a data volume, the framework can more easily support backup and restore operations, as tiny backup and restore containers can mount the volumes from the data container at any time. The data volumes can hold any data which needs to be readily backed up and restored (in the case of this framework, the Jenkins CI, or MongoDB containers).

The Volumes column in Table 2 describes the volumes needed for each Docker image. I elaborate on the details of volume preparation and usage for each relevant image alongside the details of each image below.

4.3 Docker Image Details

As described earlier, each Docker image starts from a base image and executes one or more Linux commands within the base image to create a new reusable image. The image can then be launched with one or more supporting data volumes and several additional configuration options. In the case of this framework, I use command-line options for mapping data volumes, TCP ports, and environment variables in particular.

4.3.1 Job Execution With Jenkins CI

The Jenkins Continuous Integration Server[k] (also known as Jenkins CI) is used across the software development industry for the configuration of automated building and testing of software. Jenkins jobs are also very generic, and many now use Jenkins CI for the automation of more general tasks. Jenkins jobs perform sequential steps such as version control checkouts, environment configuration, shell script execution, and many others. The Jenkins ecosystem also includes hundreds of open-source plugins which provide their own customized, drop-in functionality for jobs.

Jenkins also supports a Master–Slave mode of operation, whereby a Master server (which I am describing here) can be configured to use zero or more slaves to carry out jobs. I describe the GUITAR Slave and R Slave containers below, which are used as slave nodes in this Jenkins setup.

The Jenkins Master also hosts a very elaborate HTTP API for starting, stopping, and querying the status of jobs. I utilize this API from Groovy scripts to coordinate the parallel execution of batches of jobs, when required.

For this container, I did not directly extend the provided official Jenkins CI Docker container. Instead, I used a data volume to persist all Jenkins

---

[k] https://www.jenkins-ci.org/.

configurations. With this volume in place, I manually configured my Jenkins Master server and then took a backup of the volume. Significant Jenkins configurations included:

- The Xvfb plugin allows individual Jenkins jobs to be wrapped in a "virtual frame buffer" so that jobs which require an X11 graphical environment use a headless (virtual) graphical environment rather than requiring a full-fledged display. This headless operation was essential to running GUI tests in parallel.

- Individual Jenkins jobs can "opt in" to concurrent execution of the same job, whereby each execution has an isolated working directory on a slave container.

- Jenkins jobs can be configured to delete their local workspace (e.g., any checked-out or derived files) when starting, and to archive important files upon completion.

- Jenkins jobs can use an "Execute Shell" step to run any Linux commands, including the use of any tools (e.g., GUITAR tools, R, etc.), which are installed within slave containers.

With these basic features properly configured on the Jenkins Master, I am able to configure robust, automated Jenkins jobs for the execution of GUITAR tools and R scripts required by the experiments in this work.

4.3.2 Test and Experiment Artifact Persistence With MongoDB

MongoDB is a full-featured document store, sometimes referred to as a "NoSQL database" because it does not use SQL as a query interface or use relational database schema. In particular, the MongoDB server provides database instances. Each database contains zero or more collections. Each collection contains zero or more objects. Default collections contain text objects, but MongoDB also supports collections of binary objects through its GridFS extension.[1] Objects are represented in a schema-less, Javascript Object Notation (JSON)-like format, such that each Object has a unique ID and zero or more properties which can be primitives (e.g., Strings, Integers, Floating-point numbers), Objects, or Lists of Objects.

For the purposes of this framework, I use a MongoDB server to persist MBT and experiment artifacts. I interact with the MongoDB service itself through the TestData tool, described in Section 4.4. In terms of the base Docker image, I use a predefined, hardened MongoDB image from Docker Hub as-is and mount a data volume to a running container of this image.

---

[1] https://docs.mongodb.org/manual/core/gridfs/.

The data volume for this container provides a "data" directory which is the root of MongoDB's storage within the container's file system.

In the case of this container, I only provide a data volume for the data directory location when starting the MongoDB container. The server nor the volume requires additional manual configuration steps.

4.3.3 Code Library Artifact Persistence With Maven and Sonatype Nexus

Apache Maven is one of the most popular build tools within the Java development ecosystem. One of the most attractive features of Maven as a build tool is its integration with standardized artifact repositories which are referred to simply as "Maven repositories" or "Maven repos." Even as the build tool is beginning to be replaced with tools such as Gradle,[m] these next-generation tools still leverage Maven's repository layout and community-hosted repositories.

At a high level, Maven repositories allow Java programs to publish and retrieve Java Archives (Jars, or "jar files") by making HTTP calls to a repository URL. This capability greatly reduces the footprint of Java programs by allowing them to retrieve dependent libraries on-demand.

Sonatype Nexus is an open-source tool for configuring and serving Maven repositories. As with the Jenkins Master and MongoDB Docker containers, I leverage an existing, publicly available Docker image for Nexus. I mount a volume to allow persistence of Nexus artifacts and configuration files. I also manually configure Nexus to allow deployments by a given authenticated user and password combination. With this configuration in place, automated jobs can now push their artifacts to the Nexus Maven repository and use any stored artifacts as required.

4.3.4 GUITAR Slave

The Jenkins Slave containers are unique among the Docker containers included in this infrastructure, in that they are customized at the Docker image level rather than through data volumes. Image-level customization for slave containers is possible because of the archiving capabilities of the Jenkins Master server. Because important artifacts are archived to either MongoDB, the Maven Repo, or back to the Master server, there is no need to persist any artifacts across executions of slave containers.

---

[m] http://gradle.org/.

Both the GUITAR and R Jenkins slave images also include a Jenkins Slave Agent, a Java program used to communicate with the Jenkins Master over the JNLP Protocol.[n] This client only needs the Master server's details, which allows Jenkins Slave containers to run in a distributed manner across any available machines, which have connectivity back to the Master. The fairly loose coupling between host machines makes this approach ideal for cloud environments in particular (though we do not consider the use of cloud-hosted virtual machines in this chapter).

The GUITAR slaves in particular need to be able to run all of the tools from the GUITAR Java Toolchain. As Java tools, they can be launched with the Linux `java` command on any machine with the Java Runtime Environment (JRE) installed. They also require standard Linux utilities such as `wget`, `curl`, and `unzip` for unpacking and building software.

I have chosen to use Gradle rather than direct Linux commands to call Java tools, to simplify the management of Java tool dependencies. Gradle scripts are designed to easily fetch Java libraries from a Maven Repository at runtime and can easily incorporate inline and external Groovy[o] scripts to drive Java tool execution.

4.3.5 R Slave

In addition to execution of GUITAR tools, the consideration of predictive regression models (and potentially other models) requires a slave container capable of running additional automated jobs for construction of the binary classifier and analysis of its predictions. In particular, I use the statistical software R[P] for model construction and data analysis. The Docker image for the R Jenkins Slave includes a set of preinstalled R packages, such as those required for constructing binary classifiers from logistic regression models.

The inclusion of R slave containers in the framework also demonstrates that any such container can be added to the framework to support an arbitrary workflow step. In particular, any tools which run on the Linux operating system can be baked into a Docker image and used for MBT workflow steps. R containers can also be used for analysis of MBT test results (and analysis of MBT experiments, such as those common in academic research studies).

---

[n] https://wiki.jenkins-ci.org/display/JENKINS/Distributed+builds.
[o] http://groovy-lang.org/.
[P] https://www.r-project.org/.

4.4 Persistence With TestData and MongoDB

The GUITAR framework has long been used to carry out empirical evaluations of MBT techniques. Initiatives such as COMET [39] have sought to address the repeatability of empirical evaluations of event-based testing techniques more generally. In my observation, persistence of data and configurations continues to be a major difficulty in the repeatability of studies, especially when tools (such as the tools of the GUITAR framework or others) are so sensitive to configuration.

To combat this problem, I describe here a persistence framework for testing artifacts, as a proof of concept for proper cataloging of MBT test results. This framework can be applied across MBT frameworks and approaches, and across empirical evaluations and experiments. To this end, I implement a new tool called TestData, backed by the MongoDB Java API[q] and a running MongoDB server. Fig. 10 shows the data model used by TestData.

At a basic level, TestData persists metadata about test cases and test case executions (or simply, test executions). Groups of test cases are called *suites*, and groups of test executions are called *bundles*. All objects in the data model (suites, bundles, test cases, and test executions) can have one or more associated artifacts. Artifacts can be arbitrarily defined, but, for my experiment, are artifacts such as the GUIStructure, EFG, test case inputs, and others produced by GUITAR tools during my experiments.

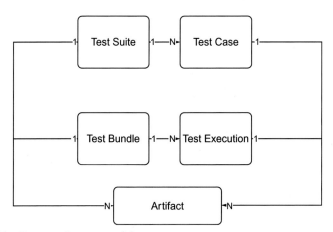

Fig. 10 TestData persistence model.

---

[q] http://mongodb.github.io/mongo-java-driver/2.13/getting-started/quick-tour.

In order to be persisted with TestData, each artifact must have a corresponding `ArtifactProcessor` implementation, written in Java. We can create `ArtifactProcessors` for each GUITAR workflow artifact, as well as processors for any additional artifacts of interest to our MBT workflow. Table 3 details a sample set of ArtifactProcessors and their implemtation details.

The current implementation of TestData focuses on persistence of the GUIStructure, EFG, and Test Case Input artifacts produced by GUITAR tools. Additionally, the Replayer logs are serialized by the LogProcessor into a simple JSON representation.

The FeaturesProcessor extracts and serializes a JSON representation of arbitrarily labeled test case features, given an existing test case input file. The specifics of this implementation ultimately depend on the features required for constructing regression models. The resulting JSON representation is generic and simply lists strings of text, allowing the implementation to easily be adapted for any desired features drawn from any desired test execution artifacts.

At an implementation level, each ArtifactProcessor implements an interface of four methods. The methods and their purposes are summarized in Table 4. A processor specifies how to serialize and deserialize a single artifact. Serialization takes a list of artifact-specific options (such as file paths or test case IDs) as input and produces Java Object and JSON representations. Deserialization takes the JSON as input and produces a Java Object.

In addition to the GUITAR artifact processing described so far, TestData also includes methods for the persistence of suite-level results and suite-wide feature sets. In the current version of TestData, these artifacts are serialized outside of the ArtifactProcessor interface, allowing them to more closely

Table 3 TestData ArtifactProcessor Implementations

Processor	Artifact	Owner
GUIProcessor	GUIStructure XML	Test suite
EFGProcessor	EFG XML	Test suite
TestcaseProcessor	Test case input XML	Test case
FeaturesProcessor	Test case features	Test case
LogProcessor	GUITAR Replayer log text	Test execution

Table 4 ArtifactProcessor Interface Methods

Method	Description
jsonFromOptions	Given a set of input options (e.g., a file path), provide a JSON representation of an artifact
objectFromOptions	Given a set of input options (e.g., a file path), provide an object representation of an artifact
jsonFromObject	Given an object, provide a JSON representation of an artifact
objectFromJson	Given a JSON representation of an artifact, provide an object representation

work with representations more natural to the R statistics tool. They are included as a convenience to support smoother downstream processing (i.e., as an alternative to performing complex processing of MongoDB objects for test case artifacts in R). The specific details of these implementations depend on the modeling choices of downstream workflow steps. I provide examples of two downstream processing methods built from TestData artifacts—`postResults` and `postFeatures`—in Section 5.

4.5 Execution of Automated Jobs in Parallel With Jenkins CI

As introduced in Section 4.3.1, Jenkins CI is a general-purpose job automation tool with many plugins designed to carry out automation of "continuous integration" tasks in software development. Table 5 details a number of MBT-specific Jenkins jobs, which can be automated given the tools and framework support we have discussed so far. With the exception of the `replay-suite` job, all jobs automate the sequential execution of a sequence of Linux commands on a single Jenkins Job Slave node. Each job calls a sequence of Docker commands, GUITAR tools, or R scripts. The Jenkins slave Docker images (as described in Sections 4.3.4 and 4.3.5) have GUITAR and R tools built in, respectively; so the Linux command steps in each Jenkins job can simply call these tools as required.

Working from the top of Table 5, the first four jobs (`build-libs`, `prepare-aut`, `build-jslave`, and `start-slaves`) automate the process of creating the GUITAR and R Jenkins Slave container images and starting containers based on these images. The `generate-random` job automates the execution of the GUITAR workflow, including calls to the Ripper, Converter, and Generator. At the end of `generate-random`, a new MongoDB

Table 5 Automated Jobs

Job Name	Description	Tools Used
build-libs	Build GUITAR TestData tools from source	Maven
prepare-aut	Build and package subject applications from source	Maven, Tar
build-jslave	Build GUITAR and R Jenkins slave images	Docker
start-slaves	Start GUITAR and R Jenkins slave containers	Docker
generate-random	Run the GUITAR Ripper, Converter, and Generator to generate test suites	GUITAR, TestData
replay-test	Execute a single test with the GUITAR Replayer, on a single slave	GUITAR, TestData
replay-suite	Execute a generated test suite in parallel	TestData, Jenkins API
prepare-data	Construct training and test data structures from posted results and feature sets	R
predict	Train a binary classifier and evaluate its ability to predict feasibility	R

database has been initialized with a new suite of test cases. The replay-suite job launches replay-test jobs for each test case in any given suite, allowing the jobs to run in parallel over the available set of GUITAR Jenkins Slaves.

The remaining jobs listed in Table 5 proceed to construct and utilize predictive regression models in R. The specifics of the prepare-data and predict jobs will depend on the models being constructed, but in our general case as presented so far, they will involve constructing training and test data for a binary classifier and using the data to construct and apply the classifier, respectively.

With these automated jobs in hand, we can build interesting workflows from the GUITAR Java toolchain and scripts which process artifacts in R. In addition to the sequential jobs outlined earlier, a framework for effective MBT also requires parallel execution—particularly during test case replay. I leverage the Jenkins Master's REST API to launch and monitor the progress of a batch of child jobs, exiting upon their completion. This distributed execution pattern can be applied to any batch of work that can be subdivided into independent Jenkins CI jobs.

LISTING 1 Parallel GUITAR Replay—replay-suite

```
static int BUILD_COUNT_THRESHOLD = 5
for(String id : manager.getTestIdsInSuite(args [2])){
  count++
  // build Map of params
  def jobParams = new HashMap<String, String>();
  jobParams.put("AUT_NAME", args[0])
  jobParams.put("DB_ID", args[1])
  jobParams.put("SUITE_ID", args[2])
  jobParams.put("TEST_ID", id)
  jobParams.put("BUNDLE_ID", args[3])


  // Use Jenkins client to launch job
  jenkinsClient .submitJob("replay-test", jobParams)


  // Wait at least 10 seconds
  sleep(10000)


  // Wait longer if there are waiting jobs
  while(jenkinsClient.getAwaitingBuildCount()
        > BUILD_COUNT_THRESHOLD) {
   sleep(1000)
  }
}
```

Listing 1 contains the Groovy code for the batch execution script used by the replay-suite Jenkins job. The input parameters to the script specify the test suite details. The script uses a TestData instance called "manager" to fetch the test IDs of the given test suite. For each test ID, the script makes a call to the Jenkins REST API which starts the single-node replay-test Jenkins job.

The final four lines in the script add delay as required to avoid overloading the Jenkins master with HTTP calls when there are no available slave nodes for execution. In particular, the script always waits at least 10 s between jobs. The script waits for additional time before submitting the next job if necessary, until the number of "waiting builds" (builds already submitted but which do not have an available slave node for execution) is less than 6 (BUILD_COUNT_THRESHOLD + 1). The script exits once all jobs for the test suite's execution have been queued on the Jenkins master.

Parallel execution can also be leveraged for tasks other than test case replay. For example, some machine learning techniques do not have the simplifying properties of the Lasso and require completely independent training and evaluation when fitting model parameters. This requirement exponentially drives up the cost of model construction and could certainly benefit from parallel execution.

4.6 Framework Summary

In this section, I have described in detail a framework for massively parallel execution of MBT workflows. The framework as described here can run any Java and R processes, but the concepts can be applied to any number of platforms which can be executed on Linux operating systems. In the next section, I show the utility of this framework in extending a GUITAR Java workflow with predictive regression models for filtering test cases for feasibility.

The framework implementation presented here is also available as open-source software on GitHub, in two separate repositories. A fork of the GUITAR Java toolchain, the TestData tool, and all Jenkins utilities are available at https://github.com/bryantrobbins, in the `guitar2` and `docker-jenkins-swarm` projects. The MBT community and any other interested parties are invited to provide feedback and propose extensions in the corresponding GitHub repository.

5. RECENT RESEARCH: A PREDICTIVE REGRESSION MODEL FOR TEST CASE FEASIBILITY

As discussed in Section 1 and elaborated upon throughout this chapter so far, MBT approaches consider context by modeling the behavior of applications and then systematically generating test cases which cover the contexts represented by the model.

From the start of this chapter, I have acknowledged that MBT approaches have some significant problems. One such problem is the problem of test case infeasibility—that is, the tendency of MBT techniques to generate tests which are not actually executable. In this section, I more formally define feasibility and ultimately use the techniques presented in this chapter to detect infeasible test cases in an MBT workflow. This provides a practical example of the predictive regression models described thus far.

5.1 Defining Feasibility

The shortcomings of automated, model-based GUI testing techniques largely stem from imprecise model construction. In the case of GUITAR, the Ripper tool attempts to construct the model in an automated way.

Because tests are derived from the model, an imprecise model will lead to tests which do not behave as expected when replayed. Due to model imprecision or other possible application-specific issues, model-based techniques often generate test cases which are *infeasible*.

I refer to an infeasible test case as one which cannot be completely executed as planned. Such test cases may provide some of their intended coverage and verifications, but not all.

5.2 The Impact of Infeasibility

Infeasible test cases introduce a number of problems for an MBT approach:

- An infeasible test case provides less coverage than designed, causing the parent test suite to also provide less than its designed coverage.
- Determining the root cause of infeasibility requires manual intervention and investigation into an otherwise fully automated process.
- Infeasible test cases cause false positives in test results, which can be expensive to manually investigate.
- Any cost associated with dealing with infeasible test cases will grow as the application changes.

Coverage guarantees are a primary motivation for the use of MBT approaches in the first place. Through coverage, the same techniques offer appropriate consideration of context for event-driven software. The presence of infeasible test cases threatens the integrity of these techniques altogether. For example, a test case $e_c \to e_p$ designed to cover `Paste` after `Copy` only truly covers `Paste` after `Copy` if both events execute successfully. If for any reason either event cannot be executed as planned, the test case is infeasible. The larger suite, if designed to cover each event within one or more prior events' context, no longer successfully meets this criterion.

Because MBT approaches often deal with very large numbers of test cases (in the hundreds of thousands), manual intervention in even a small percentage of executed test cases can take many hours. For example, consider a typical GUI-driven application, with 500 unique events in its GUI. Covering this application for all pairs of events requires up to 250,000 test cases in a test suite. Each infeasible test case could easily take several minutes, at best, to triage as infeasible or legitimately failed. If even 5% of the original test cases in the suite fail due to being infeasible, this would result in 12,500 false positives and several weeks to triage (86 24-h days, if each false positive required 10 minutes of investigation). This time due to wasted effort, infeasible test cases threaten the viability and usefulness of any MBT approach.

As discussed when motivating the need for MBT approaches in Section 1, there are additional QA activities outside of simply executing test cases. Each of these is likewise impacted due to the presence of any infeasible test cases. Any manual effort for dealing with feasibility concerns would be amplified within these activities as well. For example, with each new version of the application, new infeasible test cases could be introduced that must be triaged. For each test case rejected due to infeasibility, a new test case must be generated and executed in order to obtain desired coverage criteria.

While the feasibility of test cases can be directly observed through execution, full execution of proposed model-based test suites in order to observe and verify test case feasibility is not ideal due to the effort and computational resources required. Also, as mentioned earlier, determining infeasibility even after execution can also require some degree of manual intervention.

A *high-accuracy, preexecution feasibility indicator* would be much more efficient for the detection of potentially infeasible test cases. I aim, then, to construct a binary classifier which can classify candidate test cases as feasible or infeasible with high accuracy. Such a model would greatly improve the overall effectiveness of MBT approaches as a whole, by reducing the number of infeasible test cases ultimately included in generated test suites. Prior to test case execution, only the inputs and expected outputs of a GUI test case are available, and any such model would only be able to leverage the features of these artifacts.

5.3 Related Work on Test Case Infeasibility

Infeasibility is not a new problem and has been addressed by a number of existing empirical studies of model-based GUI testing in particular [40–43]. I am proposing to deal with this problem in a new way: through the use of a binary classifier using a regression model.

Existing research has also explored the ability to detect and fix model-based test cases that either were directly generated as infeasible or became infeasible across application versions. In 2008, Memon proposed an EFG comparison technique for detecting test cases which become infeasible due to GUI changes across application versions [40]. Once detected, one of the four repairing transformations described can be used to update the test case to work successfully with the new application version while maintaining relevant portions of its original event coverage.

In the workflow I present here, I am concerned with generated test cases which are immediately infeasible rather than those which become infeasible across application versions. Also, Memon's technique relies on the EFG model for detection and resolution of GUI changes. However, producing accurate EFGs by hand requires an intractable amount of manual effort. The EFGs produced by the fully automated Ripper algorithm are typically inaccurate due to limitations of the algorithm [6, 42, 43].

In general, approaches other than Memon's original work in 2008 have focused on the use of feedback loops (a concept first formalized for MBT by Yuan and Memon [44]) to inform models and test case generation strategies in particular about possible sources of infeasibility. My technique in this research is also based on feedback, as I use test execution results to construct the binary classifier.

Given the shortcomings of fully automated model construction, Huang *et al.*, in their 2010 research, consider the more general case of test case infeasibility [42]. Using a feedback loop, they developed a genetic algorithm for selecting feasible test cases. The algorithm starts with candidate test cases from a "seed" test suite and mutates the original suite while preferring feasible test cases. The algorithm did show the ability to converge and produce test suites of feasible test cases; however, it required complete execution of test cases in order to classify them as feasible or not. As a genetic algorithm, very large numbers of possibly feasible, alternative test cases were considered, and execution of these during the iterations of the algorithm took days or weeks.

Here, I am also proposing the use of a seed test suite to construct a model. In my case, the model is a binary classifier rather than a covering array as in Huang *et al.*'s work. I focus on the ability to extract features from test cases which indicate infeasibility rather than directly executing and observing test cases and only extracting feasibility as a binary value. My algorithms for training and prediction do depend on the ability to converge and are subject to "garbage in, garbage out" just as a genetic algorithm would be. However, the larger feature space available to my technique should make my approach less susceptible to negative outcomes.

More recently, Nguyen and Memon proposed a similarly feedback-based approach for modeling and test case generation called the OME* paradigm [41]. Under this paradigm, a starting EFG model is augmented with additional information after test case execution, leading to what the authors call the EFG+ model. The EFG+, armed with this additional information, can generate test cases which are guaranteed to be feasible.

By contrast, my approach does not focus on feedback or model updating as the OME* approach does. My technique can therefore be applied to a much broader class of applications and event-based testing domains (e.g., HTTP calls, database queries, and other event-based domains). My technique also does not depend on any particular model or source of test cases at all, which can be advantageous when incorporating domain knowledge that any one particular model (such as the EFG or EFG+) is not designed to capture. The OME* approach also depends on observing an event within a specific context before performing model updating. By contrast, my technique can extrapolate possible causes of infeasibility from a much broader class of test case characteristics than an EFG alone allows.

Finally, work by Gao *et al.* [43] addressed feasibility by abandoning a fully automated process for one that allows manual corrections. They developed a tool SITAR which suggests model and test case corrections to a manual user (presumably, a domain expert for the application under test). They also introduced a new annotation to the EFG model, *dominates*. The dominates relationship, when identified by a Ripper or manual feedback, indicates that an event must proceed another (in contrast to the *may proceed* implied by the existing annotation). In their case, they found the tool to be very effective at suggesting possible corrections for infeasible test cases.

I consider the predictive regression model approach to be largely compatible with the approach of Gao *et al.* in that I agree that additional information, whether readily presented in an EFG-like model or not, is necessary for dealing with infeasibility. The more generic model used in my research here would allow for a broader class of domain knowledge in general to be captured than an EFG alone allows. My technique requires that such domain knowledge be encoded as features to a binary classifier. Indeed, the features and annotations introduced by SITAR could provide candidate features for a binary classifier as well.

Also of note is the empirical study of Bae *et al.* [45]. Within a much broader comparison of GUITAR's sequence-length coverage criterion and a dynamic event extraction testing approach, they confirmed that GUITAR's model-based test cases began to have problems with infeasibility (what they refer to as "partially executable test cases"). They assert, as I have here, that partially executable test cases lead to redundant coverage that still falls short of the desired coverage criteria. They note that redundancy, especially within the context of a more exhaustive MBT approach, leads to large amounts of wasted execution effort.

In summary, I believe that the predictive regression model approach for detecting infeasibility can expand on existing work that considers test case feasibility. While the predictive technique may still be applicable across application versions, the direct problem I address is the generation of infeasible test cases from a model-based technique—presumably, due to model imprecision. My technique allows feasibility considerations to remain automated, and it is generalizable to any conceivable type of domain knowledge which can be extracted from or annotated onto test cases by any automated or manual process.

The idea of using an EFG or annotated EFG is synonymous in the machine learning world with using probabilistic n-gram models for feasibility prediction. Probabilistic models certainly could have additional use cases beyond binary classification; but if binary classification of some characteristic is the goal, use of a more general linear model is much more flexible. I take advantage of that flexibility to consider additional types of features in the model that I describe below, and I assert that this flexibility leads to a much more effective approach for feasibility prediction (and other predictive models) in general.

5.4 Modeling Infeasibility

As discussed in the general case in Section 3, I propose the use of supervised learning to train a binary classifier for test case feasibility. In this section, I elaborate on the incorporation of this classifier into the GUITAR Java workflow.

5.4.1 Applying Labels From Replayer Output

Recall that a binary classifier trained through supervised learning requires inputs to be labeled with known output categories. In our case, we need to label input test cases which have already been executed as either feasible or infeasible. To facilitate this labeling, we need the GUITAR Replayer to report some additional information in its test case log artifacts.

In particular, the Replayer can be updated to classify its failures as follows:

- *COMPONENT NOT FOUND*: A required widget (one required by the input test case) cannot be found.
- *COMPONENT DISABLED*: A required widget can be found in the GUI, but cannot be executed. The widget may be directly disabled or may be blocked by some other GUI component.
- *STEP TIMEOUT*: The Replayer has failed to carry out a test case event within a reasonable amount of time.
- *JAVA EXCEPTION*: The Replayer has failed due to a Java error (e.g., a bug in the Replayer such as a Java `NullPointerException`).

In all of the cases earlier, the GUITAR workflow steps prior to the use of the Replayer have produced a test case which was ultimately not executable. For this reason, I consider any such failure a possible indication of test case infeasibility. The test case that produced the failure is labeled as "infeasible" for purposes of training the binary classifier.

In terms of implementation, we can extend the existing Jenkins CI jobs from Section 4 with a job called `postResults` which takes as input a list of test bundle IDs and inspects Replayer logs for each test execution in each bundle. Test cases are counted as feasible if Replayer logs contain none of the failures for any input bundle. (Recall that a "bundle" in terms of the TestData tool is a collection of test execution results.) Test cases are labeled as infeasible if Replayer logs contain failures for all input bundles. Test cases that have inconsistent results over the input bundles are marked as inconsistent and excluded from all downstream model construction.

I also construct a second additional job, `postFeatures`, which takes as input a test suite ID and adds Test Case Features artifacts to each test case. Each Test Case Features artifact captures the set of features associated with the test case. Then, the method stores the combined set of unique features across all test cases in a given test suite in a separate object. Note that `postFeatures` runs on test case input artifacts only and does not process any execution logs. (Execution logs are processed only by the `postResults` method, and only incorporated during training and prediction through R code.)

5.4.2 Feature Selection

The feasibility model used in this study predicts a variable *isInfeas* and has a corresponding set of features extracted from test case replay input artifacts. As discussed earlier in the general case, I eventually use the `glmnet` R package to fit a binomial model on training data, using logistic regression with regularization by the Lasso. The Lasso will help with feature selection by filtering out features which are not useful, but we must identify useful features to have any chance at model convergence.

In the case of the GUITAR Ripper and test case generation based on the EFG, Nguyen and Memon show that *missing context* is the primary cause of infeasibility [41]. The Ripper, during its single pass through the application to discover the `GUIStructure`, is observing available events subject to the context of any events which have already been executed. The EFG, and any test cases generated from it, do not have the Ripper's full context

available. Nguyen and Memon go on to show that generated test cases may
have events added or removed to make them feasible.

Assuming that the order, presence, and absence of events in a test case
contribute directly to its feasibility, the model requires features related to
the events in a test case as well as their order. Table 6 shows the set of candidate features for the feasibility model used in the binary classifier for this
study.

For each test case, I extract four classes of features. I extract both *n-grams*
and *before-pairs* from the sequence of event IDs associated with the test case,
and also n-grams and before-pairs from the sequence of event types. All of
this information is directly available from the test case input files which
define test cases.

n-grams [46] are commonly used as basic features in language models. In
language models, researchers extract n-grams from sentences, which are
treated as sequences of words. In the feasibility model, my sequences are test
cases, and I propose that event IDs and types are analogous to words for the
purposes of the n-grams used in this experiment. Importantly, I am not using
a probabilistic n-gram model for any predictions in this study. I am simply
using n-grams as features of test cases for a more generic classifier.

Table 6 Candidate Features for Feasibility Model

Feature Group	Description	Examples
Event ID n-grams	Ordered subsequences of length 1–2 of Event IDs in test case	ngram_e1, ngram_e2, ngram_START_e1, ngram_e1_e2, etc.
Event ID Before Pairs	Pairs of event IDs "ex_before_ey" where ex occurs anywhere before ey in test case	e1_before_e2, e2_before_e3, etc.
Event Type n-grams	Ordered subsequences of length 1–2 of Event Types in test case	ngram_SYSTEM, ngram_TERMINAL, ngram_START_SYSTEM, ngram_SYSTEM_TERMINAL, etc.
Event Type Before Pairs	Pairs of event types "tx_before_ty" where tx occurs anywhere before ty in test case	EXPAND_before_SYSTEM, SYSTEM_before_TERMINAL, etc.

For the extraction of n-grams with length $= 2$, I insert a *START* event, which is likewise a common practice in language modeling. I expect the presence of a START token to allow the model to capture any infeasibility due to events which were assumed to be reachable from the initial application state. I do not use an *END* token, as the end of a test case should not be a source of infeasibility. For both kinds of n-grams, I extract subsequences of length 1 and 2.

While n-grams (for sequences longer than length 1) represent a *strictly ordered* dependency between events, I also add a second class of features for each of event IDs and types. I call this second class before-pairs. Features capturing these pairs are still ordered, but allow the preceding event to occur anywhere in the sequence rather than only immediately before. I only consider single events occurring before other single events.

For example, consider a test case with sequence of event IDs $e_1 \rightarrow e_2 \rightarrow e_3$. This test case would have n-grams of length 1 of e_1, e_2, e_3, and of length 2 of START $\rightarrow e_1$, $e_1 \rightarrow e_2$, and $e_2 \rightarrow e_3$. It would have before-pairs of $e_1\_before\_e_2$, $e_1\_before\_e_3$, and $e_2\_before\_e_3$.

As mentioned earlier with regard to regularization, the candidate set of features described here will be very large for any nontrivial application. The added regularization in the model should allow all but the most helpful coefficients to "zero out" during training. When selecting a model, the number of features which are nonzero is an important consideration. In general, we prefer the simplest possible model of feasibility, which would be the one capturing the smallest number of features; but we must also protect against "overfitting" to the features in the training data.

Another source of features is the "level" of each feature considered for inclusion in the model. Because all of the candidate features for the feasibility model are binary, the presence *or absence* of any feature could potentially correlate with the predicted variable of feasibility. For this reason, I include two levels for each original feature in the model used by the classifier (notated as 0 and 1 for the absence and presence of each original feature, respectively). Given our use of a regularization parameter in the regression, these features should not confound the model or its interpretation.

5.5 Working With Models in R

Once tests have been executed with the GUITAR Replayer, I import the data into R for use with a feasibility classifier. I develop two separate R scripts for loading data from MongoDB (`prepareData`) and training and evaluating the binary classifier (predict), respectively. Each of these scripts also has a corresponding automated Jenkins CI job.

Recall that the TestData tool places multiple artifacts into a MongoDB instance during the MBT workflow. The preprocessing of the postFeatures and postResults methods of TestData, as described in Section 4.4, adds a number of test case and test suite-level artifacts which simplify the logic needed for data preparation. The relevant data are stored in three types of objects:

- Results objects associated with each test suite indicate which tests from the suite are classified as feasible, infeasible, and inconsistent.
- Feature Group objects associated with each test suite contain a combined list of all features of test cases in the test suite.
- Test Case Feature objects associated with each test case contain a list of all features of the test case.

5.5.1 Preparing Data

The prepareData R script fetches relevant artifacts and converts their contents into R objects, which can be more readily used by existing R libraries for the remaining analysis. The script takes MongoDB connection details and TestData artifact details as input. As output, the script writes a binary representation of a custom R object to Amazon's Simple Storage Service (S3)[r] which includes the test data, training data, and their labeled execution results in a preprocessed format. I use the third-party libraries rmongodb[s] and RS3[t] for interaction with MongoDB and S3, respectively.

The script first creates a matrix with size N rows by $M + 2$ columns, where N is the number of test cases and M is the combined number of test case features. The two additional columns are for variables *isInfeas* and *isTraining*. As discussed in Section 5.4.2, *isInfeas* is the dependent variable for the classifier—an indication of whether the test case is considered infeasible (1) or not (0). Similarly, *isTraining* encodes whether a given test case is part of training data (1) or not (0). The remaining columns encode whether a specific feature is present or not, where each column represents a single feature.

The matrix is then converted into a data.frame object. As a part of the conversion, all of the rows are treated as records in a dataset, and columns

---

[r] https://aws.amazon.com/s3/.
[s] https://cran.r-project.org/web/packages/rmongodb/index.html.
[t] https://github.com/Gastrograph/RS3.

treated as variables. R detects that each of the variables in the datasets is categorical (which R refers to as *factors*) with two levels each. The levels are ultimately encoded as "1" and "2" by R, but this label is inconsequential for interpreting the data.

Finally, the `data.frame` is split into separate test and training objects and preprocessed for use with the `glmnet` package for training of the classifier. A helper function `loadData` is particularly important. This code prepares the training and test matrices into the `model.matrix` required by `glmnet`. The snippet in Listing 2 from `loadData` shows the construction of a matrix from an R `data.frame` object of Training data. The code uses the `model.matrix` function, with some additional options to enable the use of one feature per factor of each feature. An analogous transformation is carried out on the Test data.

LISTING 2 Converting data.frame to model.matrix

```
# Prepare training matrix
cat('Creating_training_matrix', '\n')
xm=model.matrix(isInfeas~. - 1, data=train.data, contrasts.arg =
    lapply(train.data[sapply(train.data, is.factor)],
        contrasts, contrasts=FALSE))
x=apply(xm, 2, as.numeric)

# Prepare labels
y=as.numeric(train.data$isInfeas)

# Omitted: Export training and test matrices into binary form
```

5.5.2 Selecting and Using a Model

Given the preprocessing done by the `prepareData` script, the `predict` script simply loads the parent object output by the `prepareData` script and runs `glmnet` steps for training and prediction using logistic regression and Lasso. Listing 3 contains a pertinent snippet for these steps from the `predict` script.

The script uses a standard R utility function to load the binary parent object written out by the `prepareData` script. It uses the `cv.glmnet` function from the `glmnet` package for training. This function trains several logistic regression classifiers with Lasso, and selects the best classifier using 10-fold cross-validation. Other than specification of training data, the options to this method include specifying the use of a binomial model (i.e., logistic regression) and specifying the use of classification error as the measure for selecting the best model during cross-validation.

LISTING 3 Training and Prediction With Logistic Regression and Lasso

```
# Load model as set of training and test matrices, from exported file
data <- readRDS(data.key)

# Run the Lasso
cvfit = cv.glmnet(data$trainMatrix, data$trainY,
    family = "binomial", type.measure = "class")

# Run predictions using min lambda
# Produce confusion matrix of t1 and t2 errors
confusion(predict(cvfit, newx = data$testMatrix,
    type = "class", s = c(cvfit$lambda.min)),
    data$testY)
```

The script then uses a `predict` function of `glmnet` to predict the *isInfeas* value given the features of the test data. Here, the `predict` call is wrapped in a method which produces a *confusion matrix* that includes the success and error rates of the classifier on both feasible and infeasible examples from the test data.

5.6 Summary of Experimental Results

In the doctoral dissertation upon which this chapter is based, I carry out experiments with open-source GUI software to investigate a number of research questions which more completely evaluate the utility of the above feasibility models. For brevity, I quickly summarize the findings here. I refer the interested reader to the dissertation for many more details [1].

- O1: I confirm that infeasibility in model-based test suites is a significant problem, with infeasible test cases generated at rates of 7.8% or higher for every test suite I considered, and as high as 53.5%.
- O2: I confirm that the tendency to generate infeasible test cases varies widely across applications.
- O3: I develop and train a novel binary classifier of feasibility with overall error, false positive, and false negative rates under 5%, constructed by observing the executions of randomly sampled model-based test cases.

- O4: I find that the event types of the GUITAR Ripper's GUIStructure output artifact do not correlate with infeasibility, confirming that initial model imprecision (rather than the inferences of the Converter and Test Case Generation algorithms) is the dominant source of infeasibility in MBT workflows.
- O5: I find that event IDs formed by creating hashes of GUI properties during model construction served as effective features for the binary classifiers constructed in this study.
- O6: I identify three types of features formed from event IDs that serve as effective inputs for the feasibility classifier: loosely ordered before-pairs of event IDs, and n-grams of event IDs of length $= 1$ and length $= 2$.
- O7: I find that all three of the feature types identified in O6 contributed to feasibility classifiers, no single type of the three appeared unilaterally more effective across the four AUTs considered in my experiments.

The findings above show that predictive regression models of feasibility do indeed have some utility as an extension to modern MBT approaches such as GUITAR's fully automated Java workflow. Unique event identifiers proved to be the most important features in model construction, though results about the most useful combinations of event identifiers are inconclusive.

In addition to the experimental outcomes, the work also produced some qualitative results which further motivate the utility of the various concepts presented in this chapter. The execution framework facilitated the execution of up to 60 Java GUI test cases in parallel on a shared memory machine with 256 GB of RAM and 64 cores. The TestData tools indexed and serialized millions of test execution artifacts. The Lasso technique reduced the feature space of trained models by two orders of magnitude (from initial feature spaces in the tens of thousands, down to hundreds of features per regression model).

6. CONCLUDING REMARKS

Throughout this chapter, I have made the case for the utility of regression models as the core of predictive models for binary classification in MBT workflows. In this section, I briefly summarize the content presented so far and suggest three directions for future work in this area.

6.1 Summary

In Section 1, I outlined how the broad class of event-driven software application demands more exhaustive considerations of context. While MBT approaches provide better consideration of context, they have seen little adoption due to common issues. I proposed the class of predictive regression models as a possible extension to MBT workflows, where models can be built from a subset of test execution results and used as a quick filter for desirable (or undesirable) test case characteristics.

In Section 2, I elaborated futher on GUI testing and MBT approaches, including existing academic research and existing industry tooling, relating each to the proposed class of predictive regression models. I showed that predictive regression models stood to improve on existing approaches by being more general, while still leveraging artifacts collected during test case execution.

In Section 3, I formally introduced the general class of predictive regression models within the context of the fully automated MBT workflow enabled by the GUITAR framework. While GUITAR represents only one possible framework, and I considered only one workflow, I emphasized again the flexibility enabled by predictive regression models. I introduced concepts from machine learning to formalize the construction of predictive binary classifiers trained through supervised learning and backed by logistic regression models. I further discussed the use of a regularizer, and chose the Lasso as a good candidate for regularization in our context of predictive models for MBT.

In Section 4, I described an execution framework which enables more robust execution of MBT workflows. I described how I use state-of-the-art open-source tools like Jenkins CI, Docker, MongoDB, and R to carry out MBT workflows in parallel. I detailed a number of fully automated Jenkins CI jobs which support parallel MBT workflows (and the parallel execution of Java GUI test cases in particular).

Finally, in Section 5, I summarized a recent research study which constructed and applied a binary classifier for test case feasibility. The experimental results and qualitative observations of that study further demonstrate the utility of predictive regression models in MBT workflows.

6.2 Future Directions

As summarized earlier, predictive regression models have shown some utility in MBT workflows. Briefly, I suggest that results with these models so far motivate further research in a number of directions. Here are three such directions for future work.

First, I have shown here the utility of supervised learning in model construction; but can we use unsupervised learning to learn about the nature of software without the need to reliably label our dependent variables? Unsupervised learning would include, for example, the ability to cluster observations and identify structural, behavioral, or other properties which test cases have in common (even if we know little about those attributes in advance).

Also, I find the recent work on using models to "assist" with manual activities in software testing to be a nice hybrid that counters the shortcomings of MBT model construction and verification with expertise available from domain experts. Predictive models that can suggest model fixes and potential problems with manually created or automatically generated test cases could still stand to save significant amounts of testing time.

Finally, I think that regression models can be constructed from more interesting domains, as long as reliable and abundant features can be extracted from those domains. For example, I proposed a hypothetical model for code coverage in Section 1, which should certainly be feasible to construct if detailed coverage information can be reliably extracted during test case execution. Domains from static analysis of code, which traditionally do not "play well" with MBT models, could also be a source of interesting features and predicted outcomes for regression models.

REFERENCES

[1] B. Robbins, A binary classifier for feasibility applied to automatically generated test cases of event-driven software, PhD thesis, University of Maryland, College Park, 2016.
[2] IEEE Standard Classification for Software Anomalies, IEEE Standard 1044-2009 (Revision of IEEE Standard 1044-1993), 2010, pp. 1–23. http://dx.doi.org/10.1109/IEEESTD.2010.5399061.
[3] N. Ayewah, D. Hovemeyer, J.D. Morgenthaler, J. Penix, W. Pugh, Using static analysis to find bugs, IEEE Softw. 25 (5) (2008) 22–29, ISSN 0740-7459. http://dx.doi.org/10.1109/MS.2008.130.
[4] V.R. Basili, S. Green, O. Laitenberger, F. Lanubile, F. Shull, S. Srumgrd, M.V. Zelkowitz, The empirical investigation of perspective-based reading, Empir. Softw. Eng. (2) (1996) 133–164, ISSN 1382-3256. http://dx.doi.org/10.1007/BF00368702.
[5] K. Beck, Test Driven Development: By Example, Addison-Wesley Longman Publishing Co., Inc., Boston, MA, 2002, ISBN 0321146530.
[6] B.N. Nguyen, B. Robbins, I. Banerjee, A. Memon, GUITAR: an innovative tool for automated testing of GUI-driven software, Autom. Softw. Eng. 21 (2014) 65105, ISSN 0928-8910. http://dx.doi.org/10.1007/s10515-013-0128-9.
[7] X. Yuan, A.M. Memon, Using GUI run-time state as feedback to generate test cases, in: 29th International Conference on Software Engineering—ICSE 2007, 2007, pp. 396–405.
[8] X. Yuan, A.M. Memon, Generating event sequence-based test cases using GUI runtime state feedback, IEEE Trans. Softw. Eng. 36 (2010) 81–95, ISSN 0098-5589. http://dx.doi.org/10.1109/TSE.2009.68.

[9] X. Yuan, A.M. Memon, Iterative execution-feedback model-directed GUI testing, Inf. Softw. Technol. 52 (5) (2010) 559–575, ISSN 0950-5849. http://www.sciencedirect. com/science/article/B6V0B-4XVRYKT-1/2/3c6205164e33758ee1ed58bb3a3eee6d.

[10] P.A. Brooks, A.M. Memon, Automated GUI testing guided by usage profiles, in: ASE'07: Proceedings of the Twenty-Second IEEE/ACM International Conference on Auto- mated Software Engineering, Atlanta, Georgia, USA, ACM, New York, NY, 2007, ISBN 978-1-59593-882-4, pp. 333–342. http://dx.doi.org/10.1145/1321631.1321681.

[11] S. McMaster, A. Memon, Call-stack coverage for GUI test suite reduction. IEEE Trans. Softw. Eng. 34 (2008) 99–115, ISSN 0098-5589. http://dx.doi.org/10.1109/ TSE.2007.70756.

[12] T.S. Chow, Testing software design modeled by finite-state machines, IEEE Trans. Softw. Eng. SE-4 (3) (1978) 178–187.

[13] J.M. Clarke, Automated test generation from a behavioral model, in: Proceedings of 2nd International Software Quality Week Europe (SQWE), Brussels, Belgium, November, 1998. Accessed from http://www.qualityweek.com/QWCD/QWE1998CD.pdf.

[14] P.J. Bernhard, A reduced test suite for protocol conformance testing, ACM Trans. Softw. Eng. Methodol. 3 (3) (1994) 201–220.

[15] S. Rapps, E.J. Weyuker, Data flow analysis techniques for test data selection, in: ICSE'82 Proceedings of the 6th International Conference on Software Engineering, Tokyo, Japan, IEEE Computer Society Press, Los Alamitos, CA, 1982, pp. 272–278. http://dl.acm.org/citation.cfm?id=800254.807769.

[16] P.G. Frankl, E.J. Weyuker, An applicable family of data flow testing criteria, IEEE Trans. Softw. Eng. 14 (10) (1988) 1483–1498, ISSN 0098-5589 (special Section on Software Testing).

[17] S. Fujiwara, G. von ochmann, F. Khendek, M. Amalou, A. Ghedamsi, Test selection based on finite state models, IEEE Trans. Softw. Eng. 17 (6) (1991) 591–603, ISSN 0098-5589. http://dx.doi.org/10.1109/32.87284.

[18] H. Ural, B. Yang, A test sequence selection method for protocol testing, IEEE Trans. Commun. 39 (4) (1991) 514–523, ISSN 0090-6778. http://dx.doi.org/ 10.1109/26.81739.

[19] K.T. Cheng, A.S. Krishnakumar, Automatic functional test generation using the extended finite state machine model, in: DAC'93 Proceedings of the 30th International Design Automation Conference, Dallas, Texas, USA, ACM, New York, NY, 1993, pp. 86–91. ISBN 0-89791-577-1. http://dx.doi.org/10.1145/157485.164585.

[20] R.K. Shehady, D.P. Siewiorek, A method to automate user interface testing using var- iable finite state machines, in: Proceedings of the Twenty-Seventh Annual International Symposium on Fault-Tolerant Computing (FTCS'97), IEEE Press, Washington, Brussels, Tokyo, 1997, pp. 80–88, ISBN 0-8186-7831-3.

[21] L. White, H. Almezen, Generating test cases for GUI responsibilities using complete interaction sequences, in: Proceedings of the International Symposium on Software Reliability Engineering, 2000, pp. 110–121.

[22] L. White, H. Almezen, N. Alzeidi, User-based testing of GUI sequences and their inter- actions, in: ISSRE'01: Proceedings of the 12th International Symposium on Software Reliability Engineering, IEEE Computer Society, Washington, DC, 2001, p. 54, ISBN 0-7695-1306-9.

[23] A.M. Memon, M.E. Pollack, M.L. Soffa, Hierarchical GUI test case generation using automated planning, IEEE Trans. Softw. Eng. 27 (2) (2001) 144–155, ISSN 0098-5589.

[24] A.M. Memon, An event-flow model of GUI-based applications for testing. J. Softw. Test. Verif. Reliab. 17 (2007) 137–157, ISSN 0960-0833. http://dx.doi.org/ 10.1002/stvr.v17:3.

[25] A.M. Memon, M.L. Soffa, M.E. Pollack, Coverage criteria for GUI testing, in: ESEC/ FSE-9 Proceedings of the 8th European Software Engineering Conference Held Jointly

With 9th ACM SIGSOFT International Symposium on Foundations of Software Engineering, vol. 26, ACM, New York, NY, ISSN 0163-5948, 2001, pp. 256–267. http://dx.doi.org/10.1145/503271.503244 (SIGSOFT Softw. Eng. Notes).

[26] A. Memon, I. Banerjee, A. Nagarajan, GUI ripping: reverse engineering of graphical user interfaces for testing, in: WCRE 2003 Proceedings of the 10th Working Conference on Reverse Engineering, 2003, pp. 260–269.

[27] X. Yuan, M.B. Cohen, A.M. Memon, GUI interaction testing: incorporating event context, IEEE Trans. Softw. Eng. 37 (4) (2011) 559–574. http://dx.doi.org/10.1109/TSE.2010.50.

[28] I. Banerjee, B. Nguyen, V. Garousi, A. Memon, Graphical user interface (GUI) testing: systematic mapping and repository, Inf. Softw. Technol. 55 (2013) 1679–1694.

[29] A. Memon, I. Banerjee, N. Hashmi, A. Nagarajan, DART: a framework for regression testing "nightly/daily builds" of GUI applications, in: ICSM '03 Proceedings of the International Conference on Software Maintenance, IEEE Computer Society, Washington, DC, 2003, p. 410, ISBN 0-7695-1905-9.

[30] D.J. Richardson, S. Leif Aha, T.O. OMalley, Specification-based test oracles for reactive systems, in: Proceedings of the 14th International Conference on Software Engineering, 1992, pp. 105–118.

[31] D.J. Richardson, TAOS: testing with analysis and Oracle support, in: T. Ostrand (Ed.), Proceedings of the 1994 ACM SIGSOFT International Symposium on Software Testing and Analysis (ISSTA), August 17–19, Seattle, Washington, USA, ACM Press, New York, NY, 1994, pp. 138–153, ISBN 0-89791-683-2, ISSN 0163-5948.

[32] A.M. Memon, M.E. Pollack, M.L. Soffa, Automated test oracles for GUIs, in: Proceedings of the ACM SIGSOFT 8th International Symposium on the Foundations of Software Engineering (FSE-8), ACM, New York, NY, 2000, pp. 30–39.

[33] Q. Xie, A.M. Memon, Designing and comparing automated test oracles for GUI-based software applications, ACM Trans. Softw. Eng. Methodol. 16 (1) (2007) 4, ISSN 1049-331X. http://dx.doi.org/10.1145/1189748.1189752.

[34] A. Memon, I. Banerjee, B.N. Nguyen, B. Robbins, The first decade of GUI ripping: extensions, applications, and broader impacts, in: 20th Working Conference on Reverse Engineering (WCRE), 2013, pp. 11–20. http://dx.doi.org/10.1109/WCRE.2013.6671275.

[35] J.A. Nelder, R.W.M. Wedderburn, Generalized linear models, J. R. Stat. Soc. A 135 (3) (1972) 370–384, ISSN 00359238. http://www.jstor.org/stable/2344614.

[36] R. Tibshirani, Regression shrinkage and selection via the lasso, J. R. Stat. Soc. B Methodol. 58 (1) (1996) 267–288, ISSN 00359246. http://www.jstor.org/stable/2346178.

[37] J. Friedman, T. Hastie, R. Tibshirani, Regularization paths for generalized linear models via coordinate descent, J. Stat. Softw. 33 (1) (2010) 1–22. http://www.jstatsoft.org/v33/i01/.

[38] D. Merkel, Docker: lightweight Linux containers for consistent development and deployment, Linux J. 2014 (239) (2014) 76–91, ISSN 1075-3583 ISSN 1075-3583,. http://dl.acm.org/citation.cfm?id=2600239.2600241.

[39] Z. Gao, Y. Liang, M.B. Cohen, A.M. Memon, Z. Wang, Making system user interactive tests repeatable: when and what should we control? in: ICSE '15 Proceedings of the 37th International Conference on Software Engineering—Volume 1, Florence, Italy, IEEE Press, Piscataway, NJ, 2015, pp. 55–65, ISBN 978-1-4799-1934-5. http://dl.acm.org/citation.cfm?id=2818754.2818764.

[40] A.M. Memon, Automatically repairing event sequence-based GUI test suites for regression testing, ACM Trans. Softw. Eng. Methodol. 18 (2008) 1–36.

[41] B.N. Nguyen, A. Memon, An observe-model-exercise* paradigm to test event-driven systems with undetermined input spaces, IEEE Trans. Softw. Eng. 99 (PrePrints) (2014) 1. http://ieeexplore.ieee.org/stamp/stamp.jsp?arnumber=06714448.

[42] S. Huang, M. Cohen, A.M. Memon, Repairing GUI test suites using a genetic algorithm, in: ICST 2010: Proceedings of the 3rd IEEE International Conference on Software Testing, Verification and Validation, IEEE Computer Society, Washington, DC, 2010.

[43] Z. Gao, Z. Chen, Y. Zou, A. Memon, SITAR: GUI test script repair, IEEE Trans. Softw. Eng. 42 (2015) 170–186.

[44] X. Yuan, A.M. Memon, Alternating GUI test generation and execution, in: H. van Vliet (Ed.), Proceedings of the Testing: Academic & Industrial Conference—Practice and Research Techniques, IEEE Computer Society, Washington, DC, 2008, pp. 23–32, ISBN 978-0-7695-3383-4. http://dx.doi.org/10.1109/TAIC-PART.2008.10.

[45] G. Bae, G. Rothermel, D.-H. Bae, Comparing model-based and dynamic event-extraction based GUI testing techniques, J. Syst. Softw. 97 (C) (2014) 15–46, ISSN 0164-1212. http://dx.doi.org/10.1016/j.jss.2014.06.039.

[46] D. Jurafsky, J. Martin, Speech and Language Processing: An Introduction to Natural Language Processing, Computational Linguistics, and Speech Recognition, second ed., Pearson Prentice Hall, Upper Saddle River, NJ, 2009.

ABOUT THE AUTHOR

Dr. Bryan Robbins recently completed his Ph.D. in Computer Science at the University of Maryland-College Park (2016), focusing on research at the intersection of machine learning and software testing. His research interests also include human factors in software engineering, automated software engineering, cloud computing, and container technologies. In addition to his work at UMCP, Dr. Robbins has B.S. (2006) and M.S. (2009) degrees from Mississippi State University and has worked full time as a software engineer since 2012. As of August 2016, he works as a Cloud Software Engineer for Siemens PLM Software.

CONTENTS OF VOLUMES IN THIS SERIES

Volume 85

Volume 86

Volume 87

Volume 94

Volume 95

Volume 96

Volume 97

Printed in the United States
By Bookmasters